EXISTENTIALISM IN AMERICAN LITERATURE

Existentialism in American Literature

Edited by
Ruby Chatterji

HUMANITIES PRESS INC.

Humanities Press Inc.
Atlantic Highlands
New Jersey 07716
ISBN-0-391-02890-1

CONTENTS

ACKNOWLEDGEMENTS

This volume offers a collection of papers read or subsequently contributed by participants in a seminar, 'Existentialism in American Literature' held at Hindu College, in October, 1980, jointly sponsored by Hindu College, Delhi University, and United States International Communication Agency.

Initiated, planned and organized by Mr. P.C. Verma, Principal, Hindu College, and assisted by Mr. M.L. Kapoor of the USICA, the seminar was of such a high standard and generated such keen interest that publication of the papers in book form was immediately suggested. The visiting poet, William Meredith, who happened to be present at the seminar, was kind enough to contribute an existentialist poem on his Delhi experience.

I would like to thank very earnestly Principal P. C. Verma for undertaking the responsibility of collecting the papers, as well as for active support at every stage. I am grateful to all contributors for their generous co-operation and feel particularly indebted to Dr. Kumkum Sangari for editorial assistance rendered.

I must thank Mr. Michael Pipkin, Libraries and Books Services Officer, USICA, for his interest and unstinting help in the publication of the present volume, also personally, for introducing me to the poem by Delmore Schwartz used in the Preface. The enthusiasm and efforts of Mr. M. L. Kapoor of USICA from the initial stage of co-ordinating the seminar to the publication of this book deserve both praise and thanks.

I wish to acknowledge and thank the *Thoreau Quarterly Journal* for permission to reproduce Rupin W. Desai's article, 'Thoreau's *Walden* as a Phenomenological Manifesto and Precursor of Husserl's *Ideas*'.

This book is affectionately dedicated to Ms. Donna M. Culpepper, the spirit behind the present project, as a token of appreciation, and to bid her farewell on her departure from Delhi.

Delhi   **Ruby Chatterji**
January, 1983

PREFACE

Delmore Schwartz with his delightful blend of satire, irony and humour has drawn an incisive 'character' sketch of the typical American boy in a poem called 'The True—Blue American' (1959):

> Naturally when on an April Sunday in an
>   ice-cream parlor Jeremiah
> Was requested to choose between a chocolate
>   sundae and a banana split
> He answered unhesitatingly, having no need to
>   think of it
> Being a true-blue American, determined to
>   continue as he began;
> Rejecting the either-or of Kierkegaard, and
>   many another European;
> Refusing to accept alternatives, refusing to
>   believe the choice of between;
> Rejecting selection; denying dilemma; electing
>   absolute affirmation: knowing in his breast
>   The infinite and the gold
>   Of the endless frontier, the deathless West.
> "Both: I will have both!" declared this true-blue
>   American.

Readers of the present volume, *Existentialism in American Literature*, might deliberate how far and in what respects this too too solid figure of the 'true-blue American' has encountered serious existentialist challenges in literature, as in society, during the modern period.

Though existentialism as a philosophy is historically and culturally of European origin, it has spread sufficiently rapidly and widely to have become almost a modern international phenomenon. In fact, existentialism seems well on the way to being recognised as the dominating philosophy of the West in the mid-twentieth century, even its intellectual orthodoxy. As a concrete, personalized and experience-based philosophy its impact on literature has been both substantial and significant.

Without claiming to be exhaustive, the present collection of papers explores the extent and degree to which existentialism has been absorbed by the American literary consciousness as expressed in poetry, drama, fiction and imaginative prose. Certain literary works appear to be inherently existentialist in outlook; some are consciously influenced by Continental existentialism; in other instances, analyses and interpretation of selected texts have been undertaken from the existentialist point of view to observe the results they yield. The general aim is to determine how much genuine existentialist content can be located in a particular text, to examine how this functions, and finally, to assess its value.

As a philosophy, existentialism by its very nature defies definition and abhors systematization. For the literary critic this poses certain fundamental problems, of which the principal one is the correct grasp of the various, and variable, constituents of existentialist thought. John Macquarrie's formulation that existentialism is more a 'style of philosophizing' than an integrated system,[1] is wide enough to be acceptable to the literary critic, keeping in mind that Continental existentialist thinkers tend to emphasize different areas of human experience and different configurations of thought and feeling within a broad general framework. Accordingly, no attempt is made in this volume at any rigid conceptualization or levelling down of viewpoints in the interest of a purist application of existentialism to literature. A professional introduction to the subject, tracing the philosophy back to its Continental roots, is provided by Margaret Chatterjee's paper, which helps to set the perspectives.

As Chatterjee clearly cautions, another major problem the literary critic must reckon with is the precise use of existentialist terminology. 'Existentialist' concern is not to be identified with 'existential' concern, just as existentialist literature must not be conflated with the 'tragic,' the 'absurd' or the 'literature of protest,' as these actually represent distinct categories though they may often overlap in practice.

A further problem relates to whether the existentialist outlook can be treated as a universal and timeless human tendency, surfacing prominently in periods of insecurity and crisis, or whether existentialism should be viewed in its historical specificity as a post-war European phenomenon, which subsequently caught on in other parts of the world as a 'modern' intellectual trend, even a new fashion, since, by virtue of its flexibility, it could be tailored to suit the requirements of the particular cultural milieu importing it.

The following papers reflect something of the diversity of interpretations to which existentialism more than any other philosophy subjects itself. What might seem a limitation of existentialism as a philosophy, has actually proved an advantage as an approach to literature. Conforming to the demands of particular texts, contributors to the present volume have chosen for application as their critical tool relevant clusters of ideas, themes or attitudes from the broad spectrum of existentialist thought. Wherever necessary, the individual critic's affiliation to major European existentialist philosophers has been indicated. Thus, limits have been set, the focus sharpened, the direction and scope of each paper clearly defined.

An interesting range of possible existentialist positions in literature, both creative and critical, has consequently emerged. If Chatterjee as a philosopher advises purist caution, Mulder as a literary critic defines existentialism, somewhat liberally and optimistically, as 'an attempt to reaffirm the power of the self to deal with experience'. Mary Warnock has observed in discussing Husserl, 'it has become increasingly difficult, as more and more work is done on phenomenology, and as Existentialism concurrently begins to take its place as part of philosophical history, to distinguish the one from the other'.[2] Accordingly, Desai's article on Thoreau's *Walden* as a Phenomenological Manifesto finds its proper place in this volume.

Most commentators on fiction and poetry accept the existentialist approach as a self-validating and meaning enhancing exercise; Sangari's paper, however, pointedly challenges such transformation of existentialism into a value-system both in fiction and in literary criticism.

While pursuing existentialist tendencies in American literature, it becomes apparent that fiction and poetry provide more fertile fields than drama. Since the same does not hold for Continental literature, particularly of the French school, this American maverick strain calls for some explanation. It can be only partially ascribed to the conventional distinction between literary genres: the assumption that poetry and fiction afford better scope for subjective consciousness, interiorization of experience and the confessional mode, while drama is expected to present more objective and externalized conflict between the individual protagonist and a hostile society or a meaningless universe. But Continental practice, especially plays by Sartre and Camus, exemplifies that existentialist situations can be successfully depicted in drama as the urgent predicament of man's being-in-the-world, together with the individual's crucial and terrible freedom of choice. Probably more pertinent to the issue is the natural American predilection for extracting and incorporating in literature only those constituents of existentialism with which the modern American mind can readily identify—problems of selfhood, identity, isolation, alienation, frustration—and these seem less accessible to drama than to fiction or poetry.

Two basic questions regarding the nature of existentialism in American literature pose themselves: exactly which aspects of existentialist thought have appealed to the modern American consciousness and why? how far such elements have been properly integrated or merely adapted to existing constellations of traditional American values and in the process modified, perhaps even distorted or transformed?

In the present sample survey, readings of individual authors and particular texts reveal that existentialism may be located in different densities, as also in a variety of eclectic configurations of thought in American literature. Existentialist attitudes are already detectable in American classics whose central concerns are recognizably American, like

Thoreau's *Walden* and Melville's *Moby Dick*. Hemingway and Bellow, as 'modern' writers, present a more complex case. While their fiction has been analysed and interpreted in convincingly existentialist terms, an alternative view—that existentialism tends to function in their works as a modernized guise for both criticising and upholding established American values—is also offered. That the black American writer is likely to respond to certain elements in existentialism, particularly the sense of alienation and protest, by the very nature of his social constraints, may be expected. Yet, the actual relationship, as represented by Richard Wright's *The Outsider*, seems ambivalent, if not uneasy. The existentialist stance is adopted as a cover, or as part of an ideological experiment, without being fully embraced. This is possibly because the authentic existentialist position does not ultimately promote social change through collective action: Camus distinguishes the 'rebel' from the 'revolutionary' in *The Rebel*, and Sartre hardly succeeds in injecting existentialism into Marxism.

Though American drama seems on the whole more resistant to existentialist influence, a distinction can be made between the instinctive existentialist impulses of O'Neill, whose deep-seated concern for selfhood is traceable to his Irish-Catholic background, and Miller and Albee's conscious efforts to reconstruct American versions of Continental existentialist plays by assuming relevant 'modernist' positions, occasionally postures.

In many respects America had remained insulated from the radical crisis of civilization which was the European historical experience during the early decades of this century. There can be little doubt that the two world wars and their aftermath, the total collapse of old-world values, and in particular the Nazi Occupation accompanied by the French Resistance, had fostered the growth and proliferation of existentialist literature on the Continent. For America all this was second-hand, or, at the most, marginal experience. None the less, that existentialism should continue to exercise the kind of fascination it does for the American intellectual milieu is a phenomenon worth speculation.

Evidently, certain aspects of the modern American experience make American intellectuals susceptible to the existentialist style of philosophizing. These would be factors in existing social, political and economic structures, which pose threats to the individual in American society. A high level of technological civilization with its interlocking system of urbanization, mechanization, faceless bureaucracy, large industrial and business corporations, multinationals, mass media and other means of manipulating individual lives by remote control, has resulted in vague feelings of anxiety, alienation, meaninglessness, futility, along with an acute personal sense of isolation, loss of identity, impotence, lack of freedom and contingency. The self-confident optimism inherited by the 'true-blue American,' with his faith in material progress, bourgeois conformism, the affluent society and its success ethic, has confronted radical challenges from within the individual psyche no less than from various protest movements emerging in society. The situation has been further aggravated by the pressuress of global politics: intermittent localized wars, coups, hijackings, continual super-power rivalry, and the insidious possibility of total extinction in the event of a nuclear holocaust.

When placed against the deep-rooted American tradition of free and assertive individualism—the ideals of the pioneer, the frontier adventurer, the self-made man—the need for a philosophy which can comprehend and come to terms with the peculiarly modern predicament of 'angst' and individual impotence, without altogether abrogating traditional values, is understandable. Existentialism by its emphasis on the individual consciousness, personalized values and subjective ethics can claim to offer modern man a modern form of salvation. This is evinced by its emotively loaded, quasi-religious vocabulary, e.g., 'despair,' 'crisis,' 'dread', 'choice,' 'commitment,' 'freedom,' 'transcendence,' 'authenticity'. Existentialism vindicates the individual despite his limitations and failures by insisting that he can transcend facticity in his own consciousness. By paradoxically making the ineffectual individual both creator and arbiter of his own values, existentialism allows him to retain the last vestiges of his human dignity through a neo-stoic affirmation of the self in metaphysical revolt. Sartre had declared confidently, even prophetically, 'Existentialism is a humanism,' without being aware of its repercussions across the Atlantic.

Finally, what must be recognized is that existentialism as a transplant on American culture is existentialism with a difference, having been adapted and modified in subtle and sophisticated ways to meet American requirements. Though there is currently an attempt to elevate existentialism into a universal philosophy, what can be adduced from the present volume suggests that, like its European counterpart, the existentialist trend in American literature should be viewed as a response to a specific social and historical context.

Delhi   Ruby Chatterji
January 1983

NOTES

1. *Existentialism* (Harmondsworth: Penguin Books, 1972), p. 14.
2. *Existentialism* (Oxford: Oxford University Press, 1970), p. 23.

1

INTRODUCING EXISTENTIALISM

Margaret Chatterjee

Existentialism qua philosophy, is a peculiarly twentieth century Continental phenomenon. It never caught on in the English-speaking world for reasons which are too complicated to be gone into here. Moreover it is significant that the term 'existentialism' has been bandied about in recent decades to such a degree that no philosopher or literary writer has felt very happy if the label has been applied to him or her. The term is a slippery one whose precise content is somewhat obscure. There is almost a kind of impropriety in trying to pin down something which in its various manifestations stands above all for a rejection of definitions, especially definitions of man. If my first caveat amounts to saying that there can scarcely be said to be much 'existentialist' writing outside the Continent, the second caveat is as follows. Existential concern is not to be identified with 'existentialist' concern. The former is the stuff of great philosophy and literature anyway. The third caveat relates to the occasional tendency to conflate existentialist writing with the tragic, the absurd or even with the literature of protest. Combinations of these can be found in the twentieth century, but the categories are really distinct and ought to be kept as such.

Existentialism as a philosophical movement has roots which can be explored conveniently under three headings, the strictly philosophical, the theological, and the literary. Let us consider the philosophical roots first. These are to all intents and purposes the roots of what the French philosopher Emile

Mounier once described as the personalist tree. The Socratic
mode of self-questioning and Socratic irony, are explicitly
invoked by Kierkegaard and Marcel. The vocabulary of essence
and accidents derives from Aristotle. It is the Aristotelian
adage "Man is a rational animal" that becomes a whipping
boy for the existentialists. Not only is it incorrect to single out
rationality as the core human endowment, they say, but to
distinguish between the essential and accidental is also particularly inappropriate in the case of man. Essence and accidents
are classically constitutive of substance. But how insubstantial
is man. I refer here to the technical philosophical meaning of
substance, that which is causally independent and permanent.
Let us look at the so-called 'accidental' in the context of man
and see how ill it applies. Byron's club-foot, the complexities
of marital life of Dickens, Hardy or Tolstoy are by no means
peripheral to their life-story. As for the essence-existence
distinction, this was developed in detail by Thomas Aquinas
in whose thinking Aristotelian metaphysics and Augustinian
theology were finely interwoven. To exist is to exist in act. So
although the Scholastic period is usually associated with system
building, and rightly so, it also provided the root vocabulary
of something very different, a controversy between those who
stressed essence and those who stressed existence, and which
was to have great importance in subsequent centuries.

In the modern era Descartes, a Janus-faced figure if there
ever was one, responsible not only for the tendencies which
made of philosophy a camp-follower of the sciences, but
brought into academic philosophy a stress on subjective life
which in his own country characterised a whole stream of
thinkers including Pascal and Maine de Biran, the French
'moralistes', romantics like Jean-Jacques Rousseau, through to
Sartre, Camus and Marcel. The contribution of French history
of ideas to personalism is particularly rich, containing as it
does the spokesmen of the French Revolution with their clarion
call of liberty, fraternity and equality. It is a commonplace
that the eighteenth century fostered both rationalism and its
opposite. Kant, whose *Critique of Pure Reason* was published
in 1789, can be numbered among these whose concern with
existence was to have far-reaching consequences. For Kant
existence was inseparable from spatic-temporality, an insight

that not ununderstandably, embarrassed the rationalist theologians. Kant's insistence on man's cognitive limitations left the field free for the full play of man's other powers, for example, his moral consciousness, his aesthetic sense and his capacity for faith.

It is from Hegel, however, that the more immediate history of existentialist thinking finds its take-off point, and by way of rebound. Hegel, or rather how they saw him, represented all that the existentialists decried, that is, seeing logic as the key to reality assuming that the real is the rational, adhering to a form of idealism which saw nature as the objectification of spirit, a view of history which seemed to justify the actual course of events, an immanentist philosophy which apparently nullified individual effort. Nearly all existentialist philosophers have confessed to their long struggle with idealism and the time it took them to free themselves from it. To understand why they should have had this struggle at all it is necessary to remember what Cartesianism stood for. Idealism gives the cognitive subject, the knower, a leading role in the constructing of the world. The existentialists too are people who see in the individual the key to the world. The difference is that whereas idealism in its manifold forms leads to some kind of 'loss' of the actual world, existentialism seeks above all to insist on the concreteness of the world, and this it can do only by abandoning the notion of the cognitive subject and putting the living person in its place.

As soon as one does this, however, an interesting shift takes place. The non-rational parts of man's make-up come into sharp focus. After Hegel, a series of non-rationalist, if not irrationalist philosophers, became prominent—Schopenhauer, Nietzsche and Bergson. There are very significant differences between them. Schopenhauer emphasizes the role of will in human life; Nietzsche stresses that man is a being who can create values, and the creativity theme is taken up by Bergson who extrapolates it to embrace the entire evolutionary process. All are apostles of what William Barrett calls "irrational man".

By the turn of the century another important philosopher was making a name in Germany, Edmund Husserl. Husserl was the founder of phenomenology, a school of philosophy which sets out to delineate the structures of consciousness. He

made the interesting discovery (owing in this something to
Brentano) that all conscious acts are 'intentional' or directed.
We 'move towards' not only in thinking, but in feeling, willing,
evaluating and imagining as well. This was a path-making
discovery in the light of the alternative things that had been
said before about consciousness, e.g., that it was its business to
mirror nature (Shakespeare echoes this classical Renaissance
approach in a well-known line), that consciousness was
made up of a series of experiences (Hume and the associa-
tionist school he fathered), or that consciousness was purely
formal in function (Kant). The link between existentialism
and Husserl is complex. Husserl had maintained that the
relation of consciousness to its immanent object (cf, an act of
imagining has as its object not a real object but an 'object' and
which is, therefore, definitely immanent) can only be seen
clearly if existentiality is bracketed out both on the side of the
experiencing self and its object, we would then be left with
'nostic' acts and their corresponding 'noemata'. This part of
Husserl's teaching the existentialists could obviously not
accept. They re-introduced existentiality, but retained interest
in structures of consciousness, more fascinated by their tem-
porality (just as the stream of consciousness novelists were) and
concentrated on what is *lived* instead of on what is *thought*.
Husserl saw the mind as the source of meaning. After all what
is it that distinguishes an event which can be objectively
recorded by a camera and a situation in which an individual is
involved? The answer is found in the factor of experience.
From Husserl also the existentialists derived a belief in the
possibility of describing structures of consciousness. Philosophers had traditionally dealt with judgement, inference,
demonstration, discourse. The empiricists no doubt, from the
time of Bacon and Locke, had done their philosophizing in a
somewhat inductive manner. But this programme had been
carried out at the cost of restricting the data to be described
to matters concerning the senses. This often involved neglecting
areas of experience such as the moral, the aesthetic and so
on, and furthermore was tied up with a naturalism which
seemed to go along ill with the reflective task which befitted the
philospher. If phenomenological description is reflective one
could say that existentialist narrative is confessional, a shift

which is understandable once Husserl's epoche or suspension of judgement (i.e. the phenomenological reduction) is left behind. Even the above brief sketch shows that the philosophical sources of existentialism lie deep in many centuries of western thought and no one can get very close to the existentialist outlook without sufficient acquaintance with a very rich and diverse intellectual tradition.

The second set of sources are theological. Existentialists are divided into those who take a theistic position and those who do not. But even the latter inherit a vocabulary which they may have succeeded in secularizing but which still remains strangely redolent of beliefs which they have rejected. Just as talk of subjectivity carries a nimbus of idealism along with it, so talk of crises and turning point decisions recalls a climate of thought where conversion, destiny and faith in an eschaton belong naturally to it. I speak here of concepts which are tied up with the Christian traditions since we are dealing with a philosphical movement rooted in European thought. Kierkegaard and Nietzsche between them are the two most seminal thinkers in the early stages of this movement. Kierkegaard's autobiographical style reveals a spirit obsessed with a sense of sinfulness. Remorse, guilt, fear and trembling are some of the key experiences of which he writes and they are specially associated with the northern kind of pietism in which he was brought up. The theist believes in a cosmic drama where birth, life and death are made meaningful by the great denouement of the Redemption. Passion, in its original meaning of suffering, is the gateway to the Kingdom. To the theist transcendence means not self-transcendence but transcendent Being, that is God, who beckons man to a unique and close relationship. The New Testament world-view takes care both of the horizontal relationships between man and man and the vertical relationship with God through the mediation of the Incarnation. For Kierkegaard, because of personal reasons of his own, the former was always problematic. Christian though he was, he in fact fathered the existentialism of solitariness. To see collectivism as a snare for the 'single one', the 'exceptional' man, is common to all existen tialists. The person can be swallowed up in many kinds of systems—the state, the church, the party and so on. In so far as being a Christian involves *praxis* and not *theoria* Kierkegaard spoke for all existentialists who revolted against intellectualism. The Christian sees man's contingency as creatureliness. But once the framework of God's redeeming love is rejected contingency appears as stark isolation: Heideggerian 'thrownness', the infinite spaces of the Pascalian universe paralleled by the infinite spaces between man and man, the lonely territories of the human heart. Nietzsche is very much a 'counter' figure in all this. He dislikes monkish virtues. He is clear-sighted enough to see that if God is dead it is man who has killed Him. It also follows that if values are no longer conserved in the Divine Nature they have to depend on man alone. No alternative is left to us.

The literary roots of existentialism are very evidently to be found in romanticism, not the romanticism of the Lake poets but of the great writers of the corresponding period of French and German literature. The *fin de siecle* mood of Continental romanticism hovered between glorifying the ideals of the French Revolution and despairing that anything would ever become of them. It is from German romanticism that existentialism derived the notion of the heroic wanderer. To be sure existentialists (with the exception of Camus) for the most part lost the romantic's sense of landscape. It is the human landscape which concerns these writers, and the secondary landscape of machines, concentration camps and concrete jungles that are of man's own making. It is a short step from the French *mal du siecle* (a much darker affair than the 'melancholy' to be found across the Channel) to the 'nausea' of which Sartre writes so eloquently. The sense that man is pitted against deep and dark powers surfaced after a century had passed, when the same Continent saw them embodied in the jackboot and the Swastika. There was every reason for disillusionment on the Continent after the Napoleonic Wars. There was every reason for despair in the Europe of the thirties. This brings us to the socio-economic context of existentialist philosophy.

Everyone knows that the post-war period has been called the age of anxiety. The generation that experienced the Depression, the Germany of the Weimar Republic, the Spanish Civil War, is the generation that produced existentialist philosophy. The devastation of war, the collapse of values, the prevalence of injustice, the rise of totalitarian systems—all this took place between 1918 and the outbreak of the Second World War. The dehumanizing effect of advanced industrialized economies, the anonymity of bureaucratic structures, the cries of the tortured, the smoke of the terrible chimneys described for all time by Nobel Laureate Nelly Sachs, stood out in slashing black charcoal strokes on an already dark canvas. All this, by the way, was portrayed quite literally as such in German graphic art of this period. Political realities spread a pall of terror. Berdyaev fled from Russia to Paris. Marcel worked at the Red Cross trying to trace missing men. Sartre was a prominent member of the Resistance Movement. Camus faced the realities of French colonialism. It was not a century for seeing men *sub specie aeternitatis*. Man clearly lived *sub specie mortis*.

A philosophical movement grows in a particular historical situation. This is as true of the mighty edifices of scholasticism which appear to be out of this world but were in fact paralleled by polyphony in music and the great cathedrals of the Continent, as of existentialism which at first sight seems to be more obviously of its time. But the interplay between ideas and period is a subtle one. There has scarcely been a period in history when to the profoundest thinkers of the day the times have not appeared to be out of joint. So a contextualist account is not altogether what we need. We must turn to the main trends of thinking in existentialism as a *philosophy* if we later wish to discover how or if any of this was reflected in literature, especially the literature of a country (Wall street and its happenings apart) which was in many ways worlds away from the old Continent.

We shall aim at the core rather than the periphery. This with some apology, since to do so does violence to a philosophy which abhors definitions. Existentialism above all is an anthropocentric worldview built around the central insight that man cannot be defined. No single one of the cavalcade of 'natures' which the history of ideas has paraded—man as rational animal, child of God, tool-user, spinner of words, the laughing animal, symbol-user—none of them will do, for man has a condition, he is always in a situation. But he has no nature. To be a cognitive subject is to be in relation to objects; to be a soul is to be environed in a divine dimension with a destiny in the life to come. To be a person is to be four-squarely in the actual world, individual, concrete and embodied (as the subject or the soul need not be). Human existence is *Dasein* as Heidegger puts it, being-there. The existentialists' reaction against objectivity is a symptom of their dislike of the epistemologist's way of regarding man's relation to "the external world". The philosopher's "object" is actually an artificial abstraction from the world of things to which we are related through desires, interests and other ways. For example the epistemological eye sees my room as a certain area filled with objects of various kinds. Existentially, however, it is quite otherwise. It is the place where I read, write and sleep. It is the place where there are gadgets which may or may not be in working order, books which need dusting, flowers which need their water changed, papers which blow about irritatingly under the fan. It is the context of *living*, not the *res extensa* of Descartes, still less a collection of sense data a la phenomenalism. The scientific worldview is an extension of the epistemologist's way of looking at material objects. The latter are investigated in respect of their properties: laws are discovered and thanks to this we are able to manipulate things in accordance with what we want to get done. The existentialist, I should perhaps mention, is not a Rousseauesque back-to-nature man. But he does tend to look on science and technology as agencies which have alienated man in the sense of situating him in a purely spatial world of wheels and levers where man himself is but another cog in a vast cosmic machine. It should also be mentioned that there are three other fertilising streams in German history of ideas which enter the existentialist worldwiew. One is the *Lebensphilosophie* (life-philosophy) of Dilthey according to which man is not merely a being who observes but one who has *lived* experiences (there are separate words for this in German). Man has a *Weltanschauung* (worldview), that is he orients himself according to attitudes and dispositions; he sees man and things coloured in a certain way. The second is the historicist approach which one could date from the brothers Grimm and Herder through Hegel to Spengler and Troeltsch. It would not be too fanciful to say that the existentialist carves up the Hegelian-*Zeitgeist* into personal histories, personal biographies, each of which are intensely temporal, but which are shorn both of rationality and of any ultimate eschaton. The third is the idea of alienation which comes from Hegel and then Marx into the twentieth century stockpot of ideas which are ever on the boil. It is not the epistemological gap brought about by the bifurcation of nature (in Whitehead's phrase) but an existential gulf which obtains between man and himself, man and others, and man and the product of his labours.

The existentialist does not go the way of Rousseau nor of William Morris nor of Marx (Sartre does, however, attempt a rather unsuccessful rapprochement with Marxism in the last phase of his career). Qua existentialist he tends to be rather weak on social philosophy. This is to be expected if inner experience, above all, personal freedom, is the chief value. But since commitment brings one up against others, indeed often requires us to elicit their assistance (take say a Resistance Movement situation when everything depends on what 'the others' are going to do), a man like Sartre is led from insistence on individual freedom to the strategy of group action, especially in conditions of scarcity. That drama should be an ideal vehicle for presenting the complexities of inter-subjective relationships goes without saying.

It may be useful to say something more about the existentialist treatment of consciousness at this stage, especially since existentialist novelists have much in common with the stream of consciousness writers and it may even be that in some cases existentialist tendencies have percolated into American writing through this common orientation. The point is, first of all negatively, that both existentialist and stream of consciousness writers set their face firmly against the associationst school of psychology. In doing so existentialism pits against it not so much the 'Gestalt' school as the intentional theory of consciousness of Husserl. But herein lies the canker in the bud. Husserl had analysed the noetic arc into noetic act and its immanent object. But if we single out consciousness instead of consciousness-of we are strictly speaking left with 'nothing'. This is what is behind Sartre's characterisation of being-for-itself, that is consciousness, as a *lack*, as nothing. This incomplete theory, for incomplete it is, certainly gives rise to nihilism on the face of it. The rather dismal mood of Sartre's total *oeuvre* actually stems from the peculiar twist he gives Husserl's account of intentionality. Moreover, Sartre rejects Husserl's theory of the Pure Ego which, whatever may be its defects, at least gave experience a source and focus without which it may very well be found to fall apart at the seams. Even if feeling and imagination might be possible without a pure Ego, action seems to require a central factor of some kind; or to switch terminology, the dance surely requires a dancer.

A pecularity of existentialist philosophy that has not been mentioned so far in this brief introduction is the way in which each thinker regards a certain set of experiences as the key to the human condition. This would be a point of difference *vis a vis* William James for whom all kinds of experiences are grist to his mill. It came about this way. The existentialist, like the romantic, sees experience in terms of intensity, and so each writer witnesses to what he experiences most intensely. For Kierkegaard it was the phenomena of religious life as he found it to be, that is, its heart-searchings rather than its ecstacies, that pointed up the crises of the human condition the *metanoia*, the break between the aesthetic and the ethical, the ethical and the religious stages on life's way. Sartre began by intuiting the non-existence of the imagined along with its potency, its reality. This paradox he found further confirmed in emotional experience. Later he explored viscosity, the stickiness that some objects have, and this became a symbol for him of how physical things can encroach on man's individuality (the gooeyness of the unclean table, the nail which sticks out of the chair). Marcel's root experiences are very different indeed— the sense of plenitude, grounded in fulfilling human relationships and faith in God; fidelity and hope which, though temporal, triumphantly transcend it. The Cartesian light of day is carried over into Sartre's stark vision of men and things. Marcel's sense of the mysteries of birth and death, the wonders of sudden encounter, are in a key of their own. Heidegger finds that care is the over-arching quality of all human experience. This is as different from Audenesque anxiety as it is from Sartre's nausea. The trough experiences (in Maslow's phrase) may have received more publicity in popular presentations of existentialist philosophy. But there is a very considerable *range* of experience dealt with in the novels and plays of

Sartre and Marcel, to say nothing of the philosophical writing of Camus and Jaspers. The link between them all is the quest for meaning in a world which has increasingly become opaque to human understanding and intransigent to human effort, especially meliorist effort to transoform it.

We need now to close in on the issue of the meaningless and the meaningful for this is not only a modal point where the difference between existentialism and certain other current schools of philosophy comes into clear relief, but where the difference between atheist and theist existentialists is no less sharply defined. The problem of meaning is in many ways the chief problem with which twentieth century philosophy occupies itself. But, whereas the linguistic analysts see meaning purely in terms of the multiform uses of language, the existentialists regard man's quest of meaning as something which permeates his whole life, that is it has to do with living rather than with speaking. The theist (I speak only of Christian theism) does not set off with an initial meaninglessness but with a framework in which the doctrines of creation and redemption and eternal life provide firm coordinates. Even if, as in Kierkegaard's case, the religious life is poised on the edge of despair, the theist is sustained by the belief that all things work together for good to them that love God. Kierkegaard provides a note-worthy contrast to writers like Browning whose theism may seem at times almost too robust to be credible. Kierkegaard is very familiar indeed with the dark night of the soul. The Christian existentialist, say, for example Marcel, who is a Cathothic thinker who has absorbed a good deal of Platonism, suffers as other men, but he is able to see the meaningfulness of suffering in the light of the crucifixion and resurrection of Christ.

The self-transcending movement of consciousness which is described by all existentialists acquires a whole new dimension for the theist who believes in a transcendent Being, namely God. The theist takes his stand on the 'Sum qui sum' of the Book of Exodus. This is in fact the *mahavakya* of the Old Testament. Only God can affirm 'I am that I am'. The theist existentialist finds his paradigm here. If this absolute existence (or necessary existence as philosophers would call it) is spelt out it amounts to agency, creativity in its supreme form. The

Old Testament makes it very clear that God Himself suffers. If this is so, suffering man partakes of something from which even the Supreme Being is not exempt, or rather to suffer is to partake in something which the omnipotent Being has *chosen* not to avoid. So whereas the atheist existentialist finds no metaphysical warrant for his misery, the theist is better situated in finding suffering inbuilt in the nature of things. The atheist is a bit of a rationalist *manqué* in expecting things to be intelligible and lapsing into despair because they are not. In battering against the opacity of the world and expecting a legitimation which is not forthcoming the atheist is deprived of Job's hard-won acceptance of the mystery of the Divine will. The questing self-transcending movement of Sartrean consciousness is not destined for any kind of fulfilment. While the Sartrean hero's acts rise phoenix-like from the ashes of disillusion the theist has a sense of vocation and destiny.

It is not surprising, taking these diverse orientations into account, that atheist existentialist writing should be replete with discussions of negativity in contrast to the theist's talk of plenitude. To understand the existentialist obsession with negation, and it can have an obsessive quality, we need to go back to Hegel once more. Hegel makes a big thing of negation. But he does not stop there. The Hegelian dialectic sublates affirmation and negation in a higher term. Being and non-Being, for example, are sublated in Becoming. Sartre, however, is not a Hegelian, and so negation remains in an uncompromising form in his way of thinking. Moreover, it ceases to be a logical matter and is translated into phenemenological terms. For example take the following illustrations of what he called negativities, asking a question (i.e. *not* knowing), travelling to a place (i.e. *not* being there), waiting for a friend who does *not* turn up. The critic can well say that each of these could just as well illustrate something positive e.g. one can only ask a question if one *knows* something, travelling means travelling *from* as well as to, to miss someone is in a not altogether Pickwickian sense (to students of literature one should mention that this has almost the status of a technical term in philosophy and intends no disrespect to Mr. Pickwick) to feel them present in thought.

To continue with the comparison of the atheist and theist

brands of existentialism, what appears absurd to the former appears as pradoxical to the latter and there is a world of difference between the two. A paradox is beyond the reach of reason. But, says, Kierkegaard, it is accessible to faith and to faith alone, it is faith which is able to grasp paradoxes in passionate inwardness (he has chiefly in mind the paradox of the Divine incarnated in human form). It is not that the theist has a cosy or comforting worldview and the atheist does not. Kierkegaard makes it clear that "being a Christian" is the most profoundly disturbing and illusion-shattering thing a man could ever aspire to be.

We have encountered the theme of solitariness earlier on. It is worth mentioning here a certain difference of emphasis in the Protestant and Catholic reactions to this if we take as examples Kierkegaard and Marcel. To Kierkegaard the religious life is par excellence the life that singles a man out, that gives him a vocation, something which can be contrasted with the call to conform to the moral law. He uses the story of Abraham and Issac to illustrate the tension between the religious and the ethical demand. Marcel adheres to a philosophy of participation rather than one of encounter, and propounds a metaphysic which finds intersubjectivity part and parcel of the Divine (his French antecedent in this is most notably Malebranche). For Marcel the fulfilling experiences are those where the complexity of human relationships are somehow redeemed, where fidelity and hope prevail. This is certainly one of the keys to his plays. Betrayal and failure take place, but in each case, in the very gropings of the characters towards each other, an eschaton gradually comes into view. This kind of 'rounding off', of grounding in an ontological order, is denied to the atheist existentialist just as it is denied to the dramatist of the absurd. At most the characters in a universe devoid of meaning can show a certain stoic or even romantic heroism. But, for all their essays in authentic activity, they teeter on the edge of doubt and have no intimation of an answering connivance that could provide any assurance that it was all worthwhile. On such a worldview there is no divine milieu which redeems the suffering to which all men are heir.

It is, I suspect, the atheist type of existentialist approach which is more widely known outside the ranks of those who are concerned more strictly with philosophy. But it is as well to remind ourselves that there is a very influential theist existentialist tradition and that many of the core ideas which surface in existentialist writing are in fact a secular version of what was originally theological in content. To aspire 'to exist', in some fashion surpassing the existence of *things*, is in a way to aspire to a status that can only be properly said to belong to God. I began with certain caveats. In writing about existentialism and literature elsewhere I have expressed the opinion that English literature can hardly be said to accommodate any existentialist writer in the strict sense. Iris Murdoch seems to me to write in the tradition of the Gothic novelists rather than that of the existentialists. The history of the Continent has not been exactly paralleled elsewhere. Even English romantic literature shows marked contrasts with the French and German. But the Americans had their own Revolution and ideas can jump continents and oceans.

Whenever men face new crises, when they revolt against the scientists' insistence that the real is the measureable, and when they tend to despair at the anonymity of the faceless structure of principalities and powers, the tendency arises for them to explore the contours of inner experience in quest of certitude, and out of such exploration writing which is existentialist in temper may well be born.

Short Bibliography

The Existentialist Outlook, Margaret Chatterjee, Orient Longman Ltd, Delhi, 1973.

The Literature of Possibility: A Study in Humanistic Existentialism, Hazel Barnes, Lincoln, 1969.

The Ethics of Ambiguity, Simone de Beauvior, New York, 1962.

Irrational Man: A Study in Existential Philosophy, William Barrett, New York, 1958.

2

THOREAU'S *WALDEN* AS A PHENOME-
NOLOGICAL MANIFESTO AND PRECURSOR
OF HUSSERL'S *IDEAS*

Rupin W. Desai

WALDEN was first published in 1854; Edmund Husserl's *Ideas* in 1913. A span of fifty-nine years separates the two books. Thoreau's work, as I hope to show, is an astonishing forerunner of the theoretical framework that Husserl evolved through his *Philosophy of Arithmetic* (1891), next his *Logical Investigations* (1900), then his *Ideas* (1913), and finally his *Cartesian Meditations* delivered as lectures in 1922. Thoreau's anticipation on numerous counts of the fundamental principles undergirding Husserl's *Ideas*, his most significant work, may be detected in many of his writings, but never more strikingly so than in *Walden*.[1] "Although phenomenology—a movement pioneered by Dilthey, Brentano, and Husserl—originated with the reaction against British empiricism, William James, nevertheless, played an especially important role in this movement, and the correspondences between *Walden* and *Ideas* may, up to a point, be traced back to the influence of James on Husserl.[2]

With the rise of science and technology that came with the nineteenth century, the subjective way of apprehending the world was steadily being lost. Yeats visualized this inexorable change in terms of the rough beast slouching towards Bethlehem, and it is instructive to note the several ways in which Thoreau's steam locomotive, "that devilish Iron Horse"[3] as he calls it, is its precursor.[4] Phenomenology, it can be said, seeks to restore the balance between objective detachment and subjective involvement, for it was "the rise of Nazi irrationalism [that] led Husserl to write about the 'crisis of European man', which he saw as the failure of European rationalism . . . to provide a scientific account of subjectivity and consciousness equal to its account of the natural world."[5] European thought, based on objectivism, and carried away by the success of the natural sciences, had obscured the kind of truth that a science of subjectivity and consciousness might advance. The ideas of Descartes, Hume, Kant, and Hegel are all subsumed in Thoreau's world view without his being a professor of philosophy. "There are nowadays professors of philosophy, but not philosophers" (p. 14), is his regret.

Though phenomenology has assumed many protean forms since its enunciation by Husserl—we have only to think of Heidegger, Sartre, and Merleau-Ponty—Husserl regarded his own work as the culmination of that of a long line of predecessors beginning with Descartes "who insisted that philosophy should approach its subject without any *a priori* assumptions, relying only on what is clearly and distinctly perceived as true."[6] Because such an investigation is based on experiences, no *a priori* presuppositions are called for. Whereas the physicist, for example has to assume the validity of mathematics, the phenomenologist makes no assumptions outside of his own experiences.

"I went to the woods because I wished to live deliberately, to front only the essential facts of life, and see if I could not learn what it had to teach, and not, when I came to die, discover that I had not lived" (p. 90), is Thoreau's explanation of his experiment. And for Husserl, "eidetic phenomenology,"[7] or the grasping of essences, pertains "to the realm of essential structures of transcendental subjectivity immediately transparent to the mind" (p. 6). Husserl points out that the child, for example, soon learns that $1+2=3$ is something quite independent of the red and blue beads of his abacus which are merely examples of an underlying essence. Like Husserl who describes phenomenology as "a pure mathematics of nature" (p. 7), Thoreau asks, "How could youths better learn to live than by at once trying the experiment of living? Methinks this would exercise their minds as much as mathematics" (p. 51).

Thoreau's experiment at Walden Pond is a phenomenological step toward authentic existence, "the beginning of a self that can be called his own."[8] "I perceive," Thoreau says, "that we inhabitants of New England live this mean life that we do because our vision does not penetrate the surface of things. We think that that *is* which *appears* to be" (p. 96). Lived experience for both Thoreau and Husserl is the foundation upon which an understanding of essences can be built.

The links between Thoreau and Husserl are numerous; I shall confine myself to three of the more prominent of Husserl's landmarks and trace the correspondences between these and their counterparts as seen in Thoreau's experiences recorded in *Walden*: (i) the phenomenological reduction or "bracketing;" (ii) intentionality as the main phenomenological theme; (iii) the region of pure consciousness.

I

What Husserl calls "the natural standpoint" (p. 91) is the unconscious attitude that we all adopt to the world that surrounds us and that we experience as a real palpable world that is simply *out there*. We know that the objects in the next room are there—the furniture, the curtains, the carpet. Thus the individual finds himself "set in relation to a world which, through its constant changes, remains one and ever the same" (p. 93). I am the central pivotal *I* surrounded by objects, and I confer upon them value and meaning in terms of their relationship *with me*. I regard objects as possessing "value-characters such as beautiful or ugly, agreeable or disagreeable" (p. 93). From the natural standpoint it is impossible for me to look at a saucepan as being anything other than a vessel in which milk is to be heated. My perception of it contains this utilitarian attribute which "clings" to it. The tribalist who, on seeing a saucepan for the first time, shoves it onto his head as if it were a hat is not *seeing* the same thing that I see. "The native South American Indian and I share a world of blowguns and internal combustion engines but with different degrees of comprehension of their 'essences' arising from the differences of our cultures."[9]

We assume that the world surrounding us is the same world that surrounds our fellow men. But the truth is, of course, that the fact world out there is different things to

different people. The natural sciences, on the other hand, stress
the unvarying reality of the ojbective, fixed, world out there,
and through them we endeavor to "know" it "more comprehensively, more trustworthily, more perfectly" (p. 96), Husserl
points out. Thus the natural sciences impress upon us the
inadequacy of our usual experience of that world and in its
place substitute high-powered instruments—microscopes and
telescopes—which, we have been led to believe, enable us to
understand the world *out there* better than we did before.

Without subscribing to the Kantian posture of questioning
the existence of the perceived reality,[10] Husserl's phenomenological stance would seek to question *the way it is constituted*,
the nature of its being. The ontological consideration that
this involves is directly linked up with *our* consciousness, for
obviously, it is here that the "phenomenological reduction"
(p. 103) or the "bracketing" must take place. Despite his
recognition of, and even "wondering admiration" (p. 100) for,
the utilitarian value of the scientific interpretation of the
world, for the purpose of the phenomenological reduction
Husserl discards all such standards on the ground that though
these may "work" satisfactorily so far as certain utilitarian
projects are concerned, they are not absolute truths underlying
the realities of this world. They give us *a* view of the outside
world; not *the* view of it, As Robert M. Pirsig puts it:
"Medieval men were just as intelligent as we are, but the
context in which they thought was completely different.
Within that *context* of thought, ghosts and spirits are quite as
real as atoms."[11] By means of the phenomenological reduction Husserl disconnects, or brackets, "the real nature of
physical science and the empirical natural sciences" (physics
and chemistry); likewise are suspended all sciences concerning
"men as subjects of history, as bearers of culture" (p. 162),
like sociology and anthropology.

Emerson, in many ways the fountainhead of New England
Transcendentalism, "once suggested that if a person wished to
know what Transcendentalism was he should empty his mind
of everything coming from tradition and the rest would be
Transcendentalism."[12] Thoreau, like Emerson, had recognized
the arbitrary nature of scientific theory: "The universe constantly and obediently answers to our conceptions; whether we

travel fast or slow, the track is laid for us" (p. 97). Man is a slave to the stipulations prescribed by the track, a metaphor for the established order of things that Thoreau employs throughout the early chapters of *Walden*. The railway, a product of the scientific sensibility, has altered man's world view so that he now accepts its imposition as being desirable.

Yet, Thoreau's attitude to the railway is divided: he admires its "regularity and precision" (p. 117) but warns that "we have created a fate, an *Atropos*, that never turns aside" (p. 118). The railway "rides upon us" (p. 92). Man has become so conditioned to the prevailing world view that an alteration of perspective is difficult. It is "children, who play life," Thoreau tells us, who "discern its true law and relations more clearly than men" (p. 96). And Thoreau is not opposed to only the scientific world view; he repudiates much else in the form of excrescences that civilization has produced—success, commerce, fashions. He went to Walden Pond "to drive life into a corner, and reduce it to its lowest terms" (p. 91), thus anticipating the epistemological framework that Husserl erected over fifty years later. In the experiment at Walden Pond Thoreau seeks to alter radically his (and our) perspective so that a new view offers itself to our sensibilities.

In chapter nine,[13] "The Ponds," the center of *Walden*, Thoreau gives us the concept of "the pure, real self"[14] which is symbolized by the depth and purity of the pond. In the preceding chapter, "The Village," the shortest in the book, the change of perspective is proposed after which the reader is prepared for the new world view that chapter nine opens up. In a snow storm, Thoreau informs us in chapter eight, "one will come out upon a well-known road, and yet find it impossible to tell which way leads to the village." Such alterations in perspective make us "appreciate the vastness and strangeness of Nature" (pp. 170-71). For Thoreau, Walden Pond is the point at which ths reduction takes place, for here "both time and place were changed" (p. 87), Thoreau states.

At the same time, as with Husserl's reduction, the prevailing view is not altogether expelled. This acceptance explains Thoreau's decision "to live a primitive and frontier life, though in the midst of an outward civilization" (p. 11). Throughout *Walden* there is present a dual awareness: the old life style on the one hand (primitive man as an animal living in caves, pp. 28, 37) and the modern one on the other (the railway, the post office, etc., pp. 92-4) with Thoreau choosing the mean, for "None is so poor that he need sit on a pumpkin" (p. 65). Husserl repeatedly points out that the phenomenological stance is momentary, and Thoreau tells us that he "finally left Walden September 6th, 1847" (p. 319). In general, we can agree with Buell's statement that Transcendental literature "is constantly trying, failing, and trying again to balance and reconcile the external world with the world of the imagination."[15]

Husserl, like Thoreau, began his life's work at a time when scientific inquiry with its insistence on "facts" as created by instruments had so dominated man's grasp of the world that any other world view would have seemed absurd. It was only as late as the second decade of the twentieth century that William McDougall could sense that "the 'mechanistic dogma' no longer holds the scientific world in so close a grip as during the later part of the nineteenth century."[16] The outcome of Thoreau and Husserl's reduction is that the individual is taught to look within at his own consciousness which imparts to the world its meaning, rather than remaining obsessed with the world as consisting of a set of objective and incontrovertible data.

Thus the reduction opens up a transcendental consciousness in that it ushers in a radical reflexive attitude that did not exist in the pre-reflexive world that we naively inhabited. As Thévenaz succinctly puts it, "Radicalization takes the form . . . of a *fight against the evident.*"[17]

Unlike Descartes who isolates the ego by detaching it from the world, Thoreau and Husserl plunge the ego back into the world, but in a new relationship, in a new domain of experience. This new attitude brings to light the transcendental subject as effecting a change of intentionality, a term that will be examined in the following section. The phenomenological approach is a movement toward the consciousness of the self as placed in the world of lived experience, the *Lebenswelt.*

When Thoreau in the chapter "Sounds" describes himself as being "rapt in a revery, amidst the pines and hickories and sumachs" (p. 111), we can see that far from wanting to achieve a Cartesian detachment from the world of lived experience, his reverie is an intensification of his consciousness of the surrounding world in terms of his relationship with it. Grabau's observation is worth consideration: "Consciousness is not a matter of being present to something . . . . Rather, it is a way of organizing, characterizing, objectifying, interpreting, identifying, and relating objects."[18] Thoreau's consciousness of the nature surrounding him is, as he defines it himself, "the discipline of looking always at what is to be seen" (p. 111).

II

Husserl calls "intentionality" the main phenomenological theme" because he views it as *the* distinctive character of consciousness which is viewed not as a receptacle containing sensations, but "as a stream of consciousness and unity of *one* consciousness" (p. 222). The reduction enabled us to win "a new region of Being" (p. 101), by which is meant that the world interpreted as a system of scientific thought has been suspended, and in its place we proceed to show up "simply and directly what we see" (p. 101). This attitude may be contemptuously dismissed by the scientist as being simplistic. He explains that the difference between two colours is the difference in length of certain electro-magnetic waves, or, put differently, that the "thing" transcends the whole content of the thing as perceived through the senses.[19]

The *true being* of the "thing," according to this view, "would therefore be entirely and fundamentally something that is defined otherwise than as that which is given in perception" (p. 116). For the scientist the "thing" as experienced through the senses gives us the mere "this": it is not really the *thing* which, for him, can only be denoted in extrasensory terms.[20] But "the first truth of the world," Ricoeur says, "is not the truth of mathematical physics but the truth of perception" and "the truth of science is erected as a superstructure upon a first foundation of presence and existence."[21] Unlike the physicist, the phenomenologist, as Farber points out, maintains that "as belonging to the context of consciousness, we experience the appearances."[22] The emphasis here is on "experience." The phenomenologist is concerned with the meaning of *his experience*, not with a so-called "reality" that may or may not underlie the appearance.

Consider my perception of this table: as I walk round it looking at it steadily, I am continually conscious of the physical presence out there of this one and self-same table. As Husserl clarifies, my perception of the table "is a continuum of changing perceptions," and "within the steady flow of consciousness . . . the perceptual *now* is ever passing over into the adjacent consciousness of the just-past, a new 'now' simultaneously gleams forth, and so on" (pp. 117-18). Consciousness unifies the series of different perceptions and converts them into "the thing as a whole" (p. 118). Since it is impossible for me to view the table from all conceivable angles in a single moment of time, *the table as a whole* is a product of my consciousness. Consciousness "in grasping it unites recollection and fresh perception synthetically together, despite interruption in the continuity of the course of actual perception" (p. 118).

Progressing from "thing" to "experience," we can say that an experience is, basically, a collection of aggregate perceptions of things unified by consciousness into a meaningful whole. Consciousness welds them together to form experience. "Every experience," according to Husserl, "is in itself a flow of becoming . . . a constant flow of retentions and protentions mediated by a primordial phase which is itslf in flux, in which the living *now* of the experience comes to consciousness contrasting with its 'before' and 'after' (p. 202). Thoreau's keen awareness of the living *now* of the experience is evident in his expressed wish: "I heard a robin in the distance, the first I had heard for many a thousand years, methought, whose note I shall not forget for many a thousand more,—the same sweet and powerful song as of yore. O the evening robin, at the end of a New England summer day! If I could ever find the twig he sits upon! I mean *he*, I mean *the twig*" (p. 312). Here Thoreau's consciousness notes the separate constituents of experience, namely, *he* and *the twig* which are aggregate perceptions that have been unified into a meaningful whole.[23] John Burroughs, Thoreau's contemporary, discerned that Thoreau was not a conventional naturalist, that "he was looking too intently for a bird behind the bird for a mythology to shine through his ornithology."[24] The ornithologist is occupied with the bird; Thoreau's interest is in the experience. "These experiences were very memorable and valuable to me," he tells us while describing "the hours of midnight fishing from a boat by moonlight" (p. 174). It is intentionality that unifies perceptions and imparts meaning to them.

It is in this sense that Husserl speaks of intentional experiments as acts. An act is something outgoing, dynamic. Thoreau's experience of hearing the robin, or of fishing by moonlight, is an act-character, a 'mode of consciousness,' "[25] an intentional act, for, as Zaner sees it, "it is the inherent tendency of consciousness to 'posit' or 'take a stand towards' whatever is encountered." Zaner illustrates the point well: "while driving my injured son to the hospital, a red traffic light has *for me* not only the sense of 'stop' but of 'critical interruption', possibly 'disastrous.'"[26] Consciousness is creative; it transcends perception which gives us only the perspectival aspects of things and creates experience.[27]

Every experience, as it is being lived through, consists of a series of discrete perceptions; it becomes an experience only after it is over and *is reflected upon by me.* "The natural wakeful life of our Ego is a continuous perceiving" (p. 115),[28] Husserl tells us, but I grasp myself as a distinct consciousness, as an "I," only when I reflect upon these perceivings and weave them into an experience. "It is the intrinsic nature of an experience to be perceivable through reflexion" (p. 129). Ouspensky and DeRopp call this the process of "self-remembering,"[29] and Meese explains it thus: "The perceiver not only records his perceptions but also experiences himself in the act of perception."[30] Or, as Bergson puts it, "Every perception fills a certain depth of duration, prolongs the past into the present, and thereby partakes of memory."[31] And Poulet rightly points out that "long before Bergson, Thoreau insists on the anterior *actuality* of the past. . . . But Thoreau also knows—better than most—that memory is not necessarily historical. Memory is not content simply to put us in rapport with the past; it restores it to us, it brings it alive once more in the actuality of our thought."[32]

Throughout *Walden* the impression we have is of Thoreau seeking to capture and arrest experience. Constantly there is a movement from perception to experience, toward the self-consciousness of the "I" that unifies perceptions thus redefining the "I." "Things" in *Walden* are viewed in fresh perspectives resulting in new experiences, the change in perspective being effected not by an alteration of "thing" but by a change of attitude (the intentional act) of the "I." Looking at the opposite shore of the pond "in a calm September afternoon," Thoreau informs us, "a slight haze makes the opposite shore line indistinct," but "when you invert your head, it looks like a thread of finest gossamer" (p. 186). By inverting his head the viewer sees something new, unexpected.[33]

The theme of *Walden* may be said to be an exhortation to look at things in a new way. Perhaps the most striking instance of the progression from thing to experience, whereby the "I" is redefined, occurs in the central chapter of *Walden*, "The Ponds." Here the pond ("thing"), repeatedly referred to as "it," and Thoreau himself (the "I") merge to create experience which occurs, in the words of Husserl, when "consciousness and thinghood form a connected whole" (p. 114). Beginning with the paragraph "A lake is the landscape's most beautiful and expressive feature" (p. 186), the pond is viewed as an objective entity repeatedly designated as "it": "It is earth's eye"; "It is like molten glass cooled"; "It needs no fence"; "It is a mirror" (pp. 186-88). Following this, in the paragraph beginning "The skaters and water-bugs finally disappear," the "I" predominates: "as far as I could see"; "But, as I was looking over the surface, I saw"; "I was surprised"; "I seemed to be floating"; "When I approached carelessly"; "I made haste" (pp. 189-90).

The next two paragraphs contain some of Thoreau's reflexions upon his past experience at the pond, the phenomenological grasping of one's self as a consciousness, the "self-remembering" as Ouspensky and DeRopp call it: "I remember that when I first looked into these depths"; "When I first paddled a boat on Walden"; "I have spent many an hour, when I was younger" (p. 191). By a bringing together of the present and the past through self-consciousness, experience is created.

The culmination of this movement is reached with the coming together of the "it" and the "I"—the pond as "it" and Thoreau as "I" converge: "It is itself unchanged"; "It has not acquired one permanent wrinkle"; "It is perennially young"; and, in the same paragraph, "I may stand and see a swallow"; "The same woodland lake that I discovered so many years ago"; "I see by its face that it is visited by the same reflection; and I can almost say, Walden, is it you?" (p. 193). Walden is no longer a "thing" but can be apostrophized as a person, as Thoreau himself who sees his reflection in its water. The pond is "earth's eye," he tells us, "looking into which the beholder measures the depth of his own nature" (p. 186). Thoreau's identification of himself with the pond reaches its apotheosis in the line "I am its stony shore" (p. 193), and it is here that Thoreau is able, in the words of Federman, "to achieve an identity between matter and spirit."[34] Thoreau's perception of the pond as matter has been transformed, by the process of reflexion, into an experience which is not only an intrinsic component of the "I", but also shapes its formation so that when the observer sees his reflection in the pond he is, in the language of Husserl, recognizing "the Being of [his] own inward experiences" (p. 129).

III

Walden is the record, through reflexion, of Thoreau's lived experience on the shore of the pond. The book begins with the establishment of the authenticity of the "I" as distinct from every other ego: "In most books, the *I*, or first person, is omitted; in this it will be retained" (p. 3). For Husserl the emergence of the "I" is the consequence of self-reflexion: "The stream of experience which is mine, namely, of the one who is thinking, may be to ever so great an extent uncomprehended, unknown in its past and future reaches, yet so soon as I glance towards the flowing life and into the real present it flows through, and in so doing grasp myself as the pure subject of this life . . . I say forthwith and because I must: *I am*, this life is, I live" (p. 130). Thoreau's insistence on the validity of his own experience is a dismissal of the scientist's way of looking at the world through an instrument, a barrier. Thoreau regrets that the student is taught "to survey the world through a telescope or a microscope, and never with his natural eye" (p. 51).[35]

Consistent with Thoreau and Husserl's repudiation of the

scientific structuring of the world is their preference for the imaginative constructs of art that spring from a direct experience of the world. Thoreau is not surprised "that Alexander carried the Iliad with him on his expeditions in a precious casket" (p. 102). And *Walden* concludes with the legend of the artist at Kouroo who, like Thoreau himself, creates a timeless work of art (pp. 326-27). Husserl, standing on the same ground as Thoreau, declares, "We can draw extraordinary profit from what history has to offer us, and in still richer measure from the gifts of art and particularly of poetry. These are indeed fruits of imagination . . . . Hence, if anyone loves a paradox, he can really say . . . that the *element* which *makes up the life of phenomenology as of all eidetical science* is *'fiction,'* that fiction is the source whence the knowledge of 'eternal truths' draws its sustenance" (p. 184). The Transcendental aesthetic was more concerned with stimulting the imagination than with a rationalistic frame of reference. As Kaul perceptively notes, the works of fiction written by Thoreau's contemporaries, Hawthorne and Melville, if "considered as blueprints for moral or social programs," are "idealistic and inapplicable to concrete human exigencies. But a novel is neither a plan of action nor a treatise on sociology. . . . Addressed to human sensibility, it works on those strata of man's personality which are beyond the reach of intellectual argument."[36]

Thus the subject, the "I," transcends the world of mere sensation; the world I inhabit is not merely a world of sensations, but over and above that world my consciousness has erected a transcendent world of meaningful objects, experiences, events. The transcendent realm, then, that phenomenology opens up is not one of objects but of *my consciousness of.* The emphasis shifts from the object (noema) to the subject (noesis) *and* its point of contact with the object. We must, Husserl insists, concentrate "upon the perceiving itself, or upon the *way* in which the perceived object with its distinguishing features is presented" (p. 236). Further, "he who is versed in the art of reflecting on consciousness (and has previously learnt in a general way to see the data of intentionality) will without further difficulty *see* the levels of consciousness which lie before us" (p. 288), whether they be those of experience, fancy, memory, or anticipation.

That Thoreau was well versed "in the art of reflecting on consciousness" is clear from the following account that he gives of the phenomenological stance: "By a conscious effort of the mind we can stand aloof from actions and their consequences . . . . However intense my experience, I am conscious of the presence and criticism of a part of me, which, as it were, is not a part of me, but spectator, sharing no experience, but taking note of it" (pp. 134-35). At the heart of the phenomenological stance lies self-reflexion. Alex Therien, the Canadian wood chopper, Thoreau tells us, was "never educated to the degree of consciousness, but only to the degree of trust and reverence, and a child is not made a man, but kept a child" (p. 147). For Alex consciousness and the thing-world cannot be viewed as separate entites as they can for Thoreau. Alex cannot understand Husserl's statement. "Between the meanings of consciousness and reality yawns a veritable abyss," nor can he comprehend his further statement that "consciousness" considered in its 'purity', must be reckoned as a *self-contained system of Being*, as a system of *Absolute Being*, into which nothing can penetrate, and from which nothing can escape; which has no spatio-temporal exterior, and can be inside no spatio-temporal system" (pp. 138-39). Equally unintelligible to Alex would be Thoreau's wish "not to live in this restless, nervous, bustling, trivial Nineteenth Century, but stand or sit thoughtfully while it goes by" (pp. 329-30).

Huserrl's assertion as to consciousness being "a *self-contained system of Being*" is based on the argument that whatever we call an "object" (whether it be a physical thing, a memory, or even a fancy) is an "object of consciousness," for, in the ultimate analysis, all of these are "represented within the limits of real and possible consciousness" (p. 345). Carried to its logical conclusion it follows that all "objects," being the products of intentionality (Zaner's example of the red traffic light comes to mind) can be reduced or bracketed, so that then there would "be no more bodies and therefore no men. As a man I should no longer be, and again I should have no neighbours. But my consciousness, however its states of experience might vary, would remain an absolute stream of experience with its own distinctive essence" (p. 151).[37]

In *Walden* it is in the chapter "Higher Laws" which contrasts with "Brute-Neighbors" that Thoreau most distinctively assumes the posture of the detached spectator of himself who, as we have noted, is aware of "a certain doubleness by which I can stand as remote from myself as from another" (p. 135). The title of the chapter, "Higher Laws," implies a higher consciousness; hence it is the spectator in him that can say, "I found in myself, and still find, an instinct toward a higher, or, as it is named, spiritual life"; "We are conscious of an animal in us" (pp. 210, 219). The idea of "consciousness" being separable from the physical body which is only a vehicle, as it were, is seen in Husserl's statement that "it is as properties which manifest this unity through conscious states that we become aware of the ego-subject as united with the bodily appearance" (p. 150). And Thoreau's understanding of the dichotomy between consciousness and body is seen in his speculation, while walking home from town on a dark night, "that perhaps my body would find its way home if its master should forsake it, as the hand finds its way to the mouth without assistance" (p. 170).

The movement toward the isolation of consciousness, presupposes not only the reduction and self-reflexion but, as Merleau-Ponty says, "I must even set aside from myself my body understood as a thing among things, as a collector of physico-chemical processes."[38] Since it is at the moment of death that consciousness and body part, we may well ask, "Can consciousness remain aloof and watch the body going through the process of death?" Thoreau considered such a possibility when he said, "If we are really dying, let us hear the rattle in our throats and and feel cold in the extremities" (p. 98). Because he can achieve so complete a detachment from himself, with the onset of Spring at the end of the book he can echo the Pauline challenge thrown to Death and the Grave; "There needs no stronger proof of immortality. All things must live in such a light. O Death, where was thy sting? O Grave, where was thy victory, then?" (p. 317).

In conclusion, it is instructive to note that both Thoreau and Husserl were not empiricists but theoreticians by profession: Husserl was professor of mathematics, and Thoreau, a surveyor.[39] Conant's observation on the surveyor's outlook is pertinent: "If one wants to find an activity where the degree of empiricism is very low, I suggest turning to the work of the surveyor. . . . Euclidian geometry provides a mathematical framework for the observations of the surveyor. Therefore, one can say that the surveyor's work represents an applied science in which the degree of empiricism is essentially zero."[40] Of Thoreau and Husserl it can be said, in the words of Shakespeare, that they "shook hands, as over a vast."[41]

NOTES

1. Thoreau's readings in European philosophy were not so extensive as to warrant the conclusion that a common intellectual heritage with Husserl accounts for the similarities. He had studied Locke, the Scottish philosophers, and Coleridge's *Aids to Reflection*, a work that owes much to German transcendentalism. (Walter Harding, *A Thoreau Handbook*, New York : New York Univ. Pr., 1970, pp. 111, 112, 107. See also Norman Foerster, "The Intellectual Heritage of Thoreau," *The Texas Review*, 2, 1916-17, rpt. in Richard Ruland, ed., *Twentieth-Century Interpretations of* "Walden," Englewood-Cliffs, N.J. : Prentice-Hall, 1968, p. 38). Rather, the similarities spring from a pervasive zeitgeist.

2. Husserl "credited James with aiding him in the abandonment of psychologism" (Marvin Farber, *The Foundation of Phenomenology*, Albany: State Univ. of New York Pr., 1943, p. 17. See also John Wild, "Preface," *What is Phenomenology? and Other Essays* by Pierre Thevenaz, ed. and trans. James M. Edie, Chicago: Quadrangle, 1962, p. 7). James was greatly influenced by his father Henry James, Sr. who "enjoyed the friendship of such men as Emerson and Thoreau" (Guy W. Stroh, *American Philosophy: From Edwards . . . to Dewey*, New York: Reinhold, 1968, p. 121. See also Paul K. Conkin, *Puritans and Pragmatists: Eight Eminent American Thinkers*, New York: Dodd, Mead, 1968, p. 269).

3. Henry D. Thoreau, *Walden*, ed. J. Lyndon Shanley (Princeton: Princeton Univ. Pr., 1973), p. 192. All further references to this book are documented in the text.

4. For Yeats's response to *Walden* see Robert Francis, "Of Walden and Innisfree," *Christian Science Monitor* (November 6, 1952); Wendell Glick, "Yeats's Early Reading of *Walden*," *Boston Public Library Quarterly*, 5 (July 1953), 164-66; J. Lyndon Shanley, "Thoreau's Geese and Yeats's Swans," *American Literature*, 30 (November 1958), 361-64.

5. Maurice Roche, *Phenomenology, Language and the Social Sciences* (London: Routledge, 1973), p. 17.

6. Edo Pivcevic, *Husserl and Phenomenology* (London: Hutchinson 1970), p. 13. Though indebted in some ways to Hegel's *The Phenomenology of Spirit* (1807), Husserl opens up a new area of investigation. Hegel's work is a history of human consciousness in three stages: the consciousness of objects, self-consciousness, and Reason. For a good summary of Hegel's book see Frederick Copleston, S.J., *A History of Philosophy: Fichte to Hegel*, vol. vii, part i (Garden City, New York: Doubleday, 1965), pp. 218-28.

7. Edmund Husserl, *Ideas: General Introduction to Pure Phenomenology*, trans. W.R. Boyce Gibson (New York: Collier-Macmillian, 1967), p. 6. All further references to this book are documented in the text.

8. John Wild, "Authentic Existence: A New Approach to 'Value Theory,'" in *An Invitation to Phenomenology: Studies in the Philosophy of Experience*, ed. James M. Edie (Chicago: Quadrangle, 1965), p. 71.

9. Nathaniel Lawrence and Daniel O'Connor, eds. *Readings in Existential Phenomenology* (Englewood-Cliffs, N.J.: Prentice-Hall, 1967), p. 9.

10. See in this connection Karl Ameriks, "Husserl's Realism," *The Philosophical Review*, 86 (October 1977), pp, 504-5, who argues convincingly that "it would be obviously contrary to all that has been shown so far to think that Husserl believes the mind makes things. What Husserl did believe is that things can only manifest or constitute themselves as such for a mind which is not a mere receptacle of data but has a capacity to organize and understand what is before it in terms of concepts, laws, and projective inferences."

11. Robert M. Pirsig, *Zen and the Art of Motorcycle Maintenance* (Toronto: Bantam, 1976), p. 32.

12. Paul F. Boller, Jr., *American Transcendentalism, 1830-1860: An Intellectual Inquiry* (New York: Putnams, 1974), p. 34.

13. According to the Kabbala, the number 9 "is the end of a macrocosmic and spiritual attainment, the goal of endeavour" (Lawrence Blair, *Rhythms of Vision: The Changing Patterns of Belief*, London: Croom Helm, 1975, pp. 101-2).

14. Frederick J. Hoffman, *The Mortal No: Death and the Modern Imagination* (Princeton: Princeton Univ. Pr., 1964), p. 324.

15. Lawrence Buell, *Literary Transcendentalism: Style and Vision in the American Renaissance* (Ithaca: Cornell Univ. Pr., 1973), p. 144.

16. William McDougall, *Body and Mind* (London: Methuen, 1911), p. xii. In 1935, three years before Husserl's death, Alexis Carrel, a physiologist at the Rockefeller Institute for Medical Research, wrote, "[Men] have been fascinated by the beauty of the sciences of inert matter. They have not understood that their body and consciousness are subjected to natural laws, more obscure than, but as inexorable as, the laws of the sidereal world" (*Man the Unknown*, New York: Harper, 1935, pp. xiii-xiv).

17. Pierre Thevenaz, *What is Phenomenology? and Other Essays*, ed. and trans. James M. Edie (Chicago: Quadrangle, 1962), p. 99.

18. Richard F. Grabau, "Existential Universals," in *An Invitation to*

Phenomenology: Studies in the Philosophy of Experience, ed. James M. Edie (Chicago: Quadrangle, 1965), p. 152.

19. For useful analyses of these and related matters see A.J. Ayer, *The Problem of Knowledge* (Harmondsworth: Penguin, 1976), in particular chapter 3, "Perception"; and C.W.K. Mundle, *Perception: Facts and Theories* (London: Oxford Univ. Pr., 1971).

20. Physics, as J.W. Dunne puts it, "renounces all interest in such matters as these colours . . . of which we are directly aware—matters essentially dependent upon the presence of a human observer" (*An Experiment With Time*, London: Faber, 1958, p. 18).

21. Paul Ricoeur, *Husserl: An Analysis of His Phenomenology* (Evanston: North-western Univ. Pr., 1967), p. 9.

22. Faber (see above, n. 2), p. 336.

23. Cf. William James's comment on the emotional content that is a part of recollection: "What is the strange difference between an experience tasted for the first time and the same experience recognized as familiar . . .? A tune, an odor, a flavor sometimes carry this inarticulate feeling of their familiarity so deep into our consciousness that we are fairly shaken by its mysterious emotional power" (*Principles of Psychology*, New York: Henry Holt, 1890, p. 254).

24. Quoted by Ethel Seybold, *Thoreau: The Quest and the Classics* (New Haven: Yale Univ. Pr., 1951), pp. 3-4.

25. Faber (see above, n. 2), p. 344.

26. Richard M. Zaner, "On the Sense of Method in Phenomenology," in *Phenomenology and Philosophical Understanding*. ed. Edo Pivcevic (Cambridge: Cambridge Univ. Pr., 1975), p. 127.

27. As John C. Eccles points out, "Even the most complex dynamic patterns played out in the neuronal machinery of the cerebral cortex are in the matter-energy world. Transcending this level . . . is the world of conscious experience" (*Facing Reality: Philosophical Adventures by a Brain Scientist*, London: Longman, 1970, p. 162).

28. A statement of Husserl's quoted by T.S. Eliot in "Coriolan." For an incisive analysis of Eliot's use of the statement in terms of its phenomenological significance see A.D. Nuttall, *A Common Sky: Philosophy and the Literary Imagination* (London: Chatto and Windus, 1974), p. 219.

29. P.D. Ouspensky, *The Fourth Way* (London: Routledge, 1960), pp. 108-22; Robert DeRopp, "Self-Transcendence and Beyond," in *The Highest Stage of Consciousness*, ed. John White (Garden City: New York: Doubleday, 1972), p. 97.

30. Elizabeth A. Meese, "Transcendentalism: The metaphysics of the Theme." *American Literature*, 47 (March 1975), 12.

31. Henri Bergson, *Matter and Memory*, trans. Nancy Margaret Paul and W. Scott Palmer (London: Allen and Unwin, 1970), p. 325.

32. Georges Poulet, *Studies in Human Time*, trans. Elliott Coleman (Baltimore: The Johns Hopkins Pr., 1956), pp. 335-36.

33. "It was a favorite habit of Thoreau's to bend over and peer at the

landscape through his legs, thus providing a novel (and framed) view" (Walter Harding, ed. *The Variorum Walden*, New York: Washington Square Pr., 1966, p. 297, n. 29). Paul David Johnson, "Thoreau's Redemptive Week," *American Literature*, 49 (March 1977), 26-27, in his examination of "Sunday" in *A Week* shows with fine insight how "the river bottom as well as the reflection [of the sky] are made by human consciousness."

34. Donald Federman, "Toward an Ecology of Place: Three Views of Cape Cod." *Colby Library Quarterly*, 13 (September 1977), 221. For an excellent analysis of the line "I am its stony shore" see Melvin E. Lyon, "Walden Pond as a Symbol," *PMLA*, 82 (May 1967), 293-94.

35. In *Walden* Thoreau uses the microscope only once, when he examines the death grapple of the black ant and the red ants (p. 230).

36. A.N. Kaul, *The American Vision: Actual and Ideal Society in Nineteenth-Century Fiction* (New Haven: Yale Univ. Pr., 1963), p. 46.

37. Husserl's position is closer to Locke's than to Berkeley's and, of course, he owes much to Descartes, Hume, and Kant, all of whom he salutes in passing (pp. 16, 166).

38. M. Merleau-Ponty, *Phenomenology of Perception,* trans. Colin Smith (London: Routledge, 1970), p. xi. Yeats makes the falling apart of body and consciousness a theme for poetry, most notably in "The Tower:" "Decrepit age that has been tied to me / As to a dog's tail."

39. Marcia Moss, ed. "A Catalog of Thoreau's Surveys in the Concord Free Public Library," *Thoreau Society Booklet* 28 (Geneseo, New York: The Thoreau Society, 1976), p.3.

40. James B. Conant, *Modern Science and Modern Man* (Garden City, New York: Doubleday, 1953), pp. 42-43.

41. *The Winter's Tale*, I,i,30.

3

ALONE AND HARD BESET: EXISTENTIAL GLIMPSES OF AMERICAN WOMEN POETS

William Mulder

I take my title from a poem by Elinor Wylie.   It reads:

Now let no charitable hope
Confuse my mind with images
Of eagle and of antelope:
I am in nature none of these.

I was, being human, born alone;
I am, being woman, hard beset;
I live by squeezing from a stone
The little nourishment I get.

In masks outrageous and austere
The years go by in single file;
But none has merited my fear,
And none has quite escaped my smile.[1]

"Alone and hard beset": nowhere is the double jeopardy of being human and a woman better described, nor with greater independence.   Miss Wylie's persona speaks like an emancipated woman, not a woman liberated from the burdens of either her humanity or her womanhood but a woman redefining her existential situation in her own terms, having it out, as Adrienne Rich says of Emily Dickinson, "on her own premises."   This is not the voice of either metaphysical or social rebellion but of acceptance of the human condition and the givens of her life as a woman.   It is an acceptance with a difference, however, a declaration that, as woman and as poet, she is trying to cope.

I could call my paper "Learning to Cope," because central to my exposition is that "existentialism can be thought of as an attempt to reaffirm the power of the self to deal with experience,"[2] however hazardous and contingent.

> I stepped from Plank to Plank
> A slow and cautious way
> The Stars about my Head I felt
> About my Feet the Sea.
>
> I knew not but the next
> Would be my final inch—
> This gave me that precarious Gait
> Some call Experience.

You recognize that voice. It is Emily Dickinson, in so many ways the spiritual ancestor of this generation's American women poets, source of a divided stream of inspiration and influence that includes the cerebral writers like Marianne Moore and May Swenson on the one hand and the confessional, subjective, and therefore more existential writers like Sylvia Plath, Anne Sexton, Adrienne Rich, Denise Levertov and an explosive handful of Black activists on the other—all women who, having made the discovery that they exist, have felt both the stars above their heads and the sea about their feet and probe experience with Dickinson's sense of perpetual crisis and possibility: "My Life had stood, a Loaded Gun." "*I live*," they say, "therefore I *am*," and seem ready, with Heidegger, that philosopher of extremes, to "Risk all, lose all."[3] "No more masks!" says Muriel Rukeyser, "No more mythologies!"[4]

One of the myths, of course, is that women are supposed to seek fulfilment in bed, not in books, that their world is the world of "kinder, kuche, kirche"—of children, kitchen, and the church. Anne Bradstreet, 17th century New England colonial housewife who wrote poetry on the sly and who felt safer in her husband the Governor's arms, than in the hard embrace of Calvinism, had her troubles with carping neighbours who thought her hand "a needle better fits"—though she persisted as we know and won praise as "the Tenth Muse

Lately Sprung up in America." Dr. Samuel Johnson, that
curmudgeon, despatched aspiring women with an anecdote:
upon hearing a woman preacher he was reminded, he said, of
a dog dancing on its hind legs; one marvels not at how well it
is done, but that it is done at all.[5]   Amy Lowell, the American
impresario of Imagism (or Amygism) and in her own way quite
as formidable as Dr. Johnson, had to acknowledge the preju-
dice in her own day:

> Taking us by and large, we're a queer lot
> We women who write poetry . . . .
> I wonder what it is that makes us do it,
> Singles us out to scribble down, man-wise,
> The fragments of ourselves.   Why are we
> Already mother-creatures, double-bearing,
> With matrices in body and in brain?

Erica Jong puts that double-bearing biological image (so
inevitable in describing female creativity) in current Black
vernacular in "Bitter Pills for the Dark Ladies":

> Jus' remember you got no rights.   Anything go wrong
> they gonna roun' you up & howl "Poetess!"
> (sorta like "Nigra!") then kick the shit outa you
> sayin': You got Natural Rhythm (28 days)
> so why you wanna mess aroun'?

(That poem was motivated, by the way, by Robert Lowell's
remark about Sylvia Plath, "—hardly a person at all, or a
woman, certainly not another 'poetess,' but . . .")
    "Natural Rhythm." Today's feminists tear the notion that
"biology is destiny" apart: "The fault lies not in our stars,
our hormones, our menstrual cycles or our empty internal
spaces, but in our institutions and in our education.   I am not
real," they say, "to my civilization. I am not real to the culture
that has spawned me and has made use of me. I am only a
collection of myths. I am an existential stand-in. The *idea*
of me is real—the temptress, the goddess, the child, the
mother—but *I* am not real."[6]
    The unexamined life, said Socrates, is not worth living.

The inauthentic life, say the existentialists, is not worth examining. Until she slammed the door at the end of *A Doll's House*, Nora Holm's life was inauthentic. A life of surfaces prescribed by custom and circumstance rather than inner compulsion is not *real*, is not authentic. Carolyn Kizer calls the real life of women the "world's best-kept secret; . . . the private lives of one-half of humanity."[7] Today's women poets are its custodians and confessors who have turned the doll's house into a glass house for all the world to look in and view the invisible lives of the women within. They are retelling the story of Adam and Eve from Eve's point of view, of Leda and the Swan from Leda's point of view, of Jason and Medea from Medea's point of view, of fathers and daughters from the daughters' point of view; they are describing and dissecting the life inside the cage, behind the veil, under the bell jar, from precisely *that* vantage point of inner space, the space most sacred to the existentialists.

In these private lives writ large the women poets have found a "will to change" as they search for significance in daily existence and try out their redefinitions of what it means to be a woman *and* a writer (a wife *and*, a mother *and*, a lover *and*, a daughter *and* a poet). They do not ask Elizabeth Barrett Browning's doting question, "How do I love thee?" but rather the daring question Eve might have asked after the Fall: "What can I make of my situation? Let me count the ways." It is an existential inquiry suited, if I may be excused the sexism, suited to the feminine poetic consciousness, by which I do not mean the sensibility of the Lady poets (who, as someone has meanly remarked, got their mental hysterectomies early) but the sensibility of Psyche, the Greek personification of mind, of soul, the complement of Eros. The muse, remember, was always a woman, though the poet was a man. We need not expunge "feminine" and "masculine" from our vocabulary: they are convenient shorthand for the distinctive qualities that constitute an ideal androgyny. Given their givens, their sensibility however you want to label it, women may be seen as natural existentialists, and women poets as endowed to advantage to probe and describe experience in the concrete, contingent, and subjective manner we associate with the existential mode. Existentialism abhors rational systems and abstractions as nature abhors a vacuum; it prefers to fill the void of theoretical being with the particulars of subjective daily existence, a consciousness of self, and of the willingness of that self, pulsing and palpable, to assume responsibility for its own humanity, creating its own world, and achieving authenticity. It is a work of reconstruction, of "diving into the wreck," Adrienne Rich's startling metaphor for the recovery of self. The rehabilitation of the ego, not of its dissolution as in Prufrock, is a task for awakened women, not for hollow men. In its search for wholeness and self-fulfilment for women, feminism—not as program but as outlook—may be the humanism of our times and to that extent runs in the same channel with existentialism. Sartre, you may remember, once defined existentialism as humanism (although someone has argued that humanism only makes one a sensitized outsider). With a different set of the sail, the women manage a different tack with the same winds of change that threaten the male ego with shipwreck. Paradoxically, a sense of community emerges from such an intensely private pursuit of self: a mystique of sisterhood (as good a word as brotherhood), the shock of recognition of redefined selves creatively fulfilled replacing the "feminine mystique" of yesteryear, by now discredited, which had enabled women to rationalize, romanticize, and idealize their subservient position in a man's world.

The women poets are natural existentialists in Simone de Beauvoir's sense: "There are two ways," she says, "of seizing and explaining metaphysical reality. On can attempt to elucidate the universal signification in an abstract language. In this case the theory takes a universal and timeless form. Subjectivity and historicity are utterly excluded. One can incorporate into the doctrine the concrete and dramatic aspect of experience and propose not some abstract truth, but *my truth as I realize it in my own life*. This is the existentialistic way," she says. "And this also explains why existentialism often chooses to express itself through fiction, novel and play. . . . The purpose is to grasp existence in the act itself, in which it fulfils itself."[8]

The very titles of so many poems by women capture that sense of grasping existence in the self-fulfilling act itself: Denise Levertov's "O Taste and See," Adrienne Rich's "Snapshots of a Daughter-in-Law," Anne Sexton's "Pain for a Daughter," Sylvia Plath's "Black Rook in Rainy Weather," Margaret Atwood's "It is Dangerous to Read Newspapers," Gwendolyn Brooks' "Riot," May Swenson's "At Breakfast," Marianne Moore's "To a Steam Roller"—all poems with real toads in their imaginary gardens. In such poems, existence does indeed precede essence, that is, there is "no pre-established, basically ontological pattern of human nature, no truly objective point of view, no reality in mankind, only living men and women."[9] "The one meaningful point of reference for any individual," says Hazel Barnes, "is his own immediate consciousness. The living person in his totality of rational, physical and emotional reactions is an irreducible factor. He cannot be confined in systems."[10] That's why we are all ready, at times, to fly over the cuckoo's nest. That is the overwhelming sense of these poems by and so often about women: the great liberating theme, the expanded subject matter, is the poets' removing one mask and trying on another, stepping out of one convention and into another, out of one institution and into another, retreating in and out of madness, flirting with death and taboos, moving out, looking back, walking around, going up, coming down. They give the lie to Theodore Roethke's complaint about women poets, whose range in subject matter and emotional tone, he felt, was limited and who lacked a sense of humor, charges trailing a long list of minor "aesthetic and moral shortcomings" he found in them:

> the spinning-out; the embroidering of trivial themes; a concern with the mere surfaces of life—that special province of the feminine talent in prose—hiding from the real agonies of the spirit; refusing to face up to what existence is; lyric or religious posturing; running between the boudoir and the altar, stamping a tiny foot against God; or lapsing into a sententiousness that implies the author has re-invented integrity; carrying on excessively about Fate, about time; lamenting the lot of woman; caterwauling; writing the same poem about fifty times, and so on.[11]

That might have been true of the Edna St. Vincent Millays and Greenwich Village before *Village Voice*. It's not true of the women we are talking about. Their subject more often than not is the invisible woman caught in the cage of domesticity and inventing daily strategies to keep madness like a wolf from the door or to resist the blandishments of that ultimate lover Death.

> I tie my Hat—I crease my Shawl—
> Life's little duties do—precisely—
> As the very least
> Were infinite to me—
>
> . . .
>
> Therefore—we do life's labor—
> Though life's Reward—be done—
> With scrupulous exactness—
> To hold our Senses—on.

That was Emily Dickinson's prescription for survival, investing the trivial, the daily, the factual with existential value, hanging on, staying in there, and not in the name of any great abstraction but in the name of what is immediate and palpable, the infinity of the very least, the efficacy of routine, which may prove more ineffable than mystery.

"Life's labor" for the woman who is also a poet, the labor "to hold one's senses on," is the act of writing itself, congenially existential as a creative and transforming, even self-transcending, exercise, but fraught with psychic hazards when those labors exhaust on the one hand or exhilarate (accelarate) out of control on the other. Sylvia Plath's consuming hatred of a world she never made finally consumed her. Her labors as housewife and poet both undid her. The warnings are everywhere in the poetry that became a bloodjet not to be stopped. In "Lesbos" the domestic imagery is all repugnant: "Viciousness in the kitchen:/The potatoes hiss." The child face down on the floor is a "Little unstrung puppet, kicking to disappear . . . ./She'll cut her throat at ten if she's mad at two./The baby smiles, fat snail . . . ./Meanwhile there's a stink of fat and baby crap./I'm doped and thick from my last sleeping pill./The smog of cooking, the smog of hell/Floats our heads, two venomous opposites,/ . . . ."

> Now I am silent, hate
> Up to my neck,
> Thick, thick.
> I do not speak.
> I am packing the hard potatoes like good clothes,
> I am packing the babies,
> I am packing the sick cats . . . .
>
> You peer from the door,
> Sad hag. "Every woman's a whore.
> I can't communicate."
> I see your cute decor
> Close on you like the fist of a baby
> Or an anemone, that sea
> Sweetheart, that kleptomaniac.
> I am still raw.
> I say I may be back.
> You know what lies are for.

In Plath we have a poetry of cruelty as in Artaud we have a theatre of cruelty.

Anne Sexton, who eventually followed Plath in self-destruction, is less overwrought in her domestic scenes:

> Some women marry houses.
> It's another kind of skin; it has a heart,
>   a mouth, a liver and bowel movements.
> The walls are permanent and pink.
>
> See how she sits on her knees all day,
>   faithfully washing herself down.
> Men enter by force, drawn back like Jonah
>   into their fleshy mothers.
> A woman *is* her mother.
> That's the main thing.

Poems about being a woman are of course common in the feminine repertory, but far from commonplace. For a change we see women as they see themselves and as they react to how others see them or have seen them, going back to Sappho, as in Carolyn Kizer's "Pro Femina":

From Sappho to myself, consider the fate of women.
How unwomanly to discuss it ! Like a noose or an albatross
      necktie.
The clinical sobriquet hangs us: cod-piece coveters.
Never mind these epithets; I myself have collected some
      honeys.
. . . .

While men have politely debated free will (she says), we
      have howled for it,
Howl still, pacing the centuries . . . . I'm aware there were
      millions
Of mutes for every Saint Joan or sainted Jane Austen,
Who, vague-eyed and acquiescent, worshipped God as a man.
I'm not concerned with those cabbageheads not truly
      feminine
But neutered by labor.   I mean real women, like *you* and
      like *me*.

Later in the poem, which I find so reminiscent of the voice
and manner of the Roman satirist Propertius, Miss Kizer,
taking "The Independent Woman" as her theme, admits that
women, as do men, "need dependency," sometimes, "cosseting
and well-treatment":

We will be cows for a while, because babies howl for us,
Be kittens or bitches, who want to eat grass now and then
For the sake of our health. But the role of pastoral
      heroine
Is not permanent, Jack. We want to get back to the
      meeting.

Adrienne Rich describes how, "piece by piece" she seemed
"to re-enter the world" in successive stages in her development:

whole biographies swam up and
swallowed me like Jonah.

At one stage she learned to make herself

unappetizing.   Scaly as a dry bulb
thrown into a cellar

naming "over the bare necessities" until "practice" would
make her "middling perfect" and she would "dare inhabit the
world again," a sort of feminine Notes from the Underground.

> I have invitations:
> a curl of mist steams upward
>
> from a field, visible as my breath,
> houses along a road stand waiting
>
> like old women knitting, breathless
> to tell their tales.

These are not repudiations of traditional roles so much as
critical reappraisals. That is true of Denise Levertov's
"Stepping Westward":

> . . . .
> If a woman is inconstant,
> good, I am faithful to
>
> ebb and flow, I fall
> in season and now
>
> is a time of ripening
> If her part
>
> is to be true
> a north star,
>
> good, I hold steady
> in the black sky
>
> and vanish by day,
> yet burn there
>
> in blue or above
> quilts of cloud.
>
> There is no savor
> more sweet, more salt
>
> than to be glad to be
> what, woman,
>
> and who, myself,
> I am, a shadow

that grows longer as the sun
moves, drawn out

on a thread of wonder.
If I bear burdens

They begin to be remembered
as gifts, goods, a basket

of bread that hurts
my shoulders but closes me

in fragrance. I can
eat as I go.

There's a startling, and I would argue, existential rehandling of
the stereotype of the eternal triangle in Anne Sexton's "For
My Lover Returning to His Wife," which deserves reading in
full:

She is all there.
She was melted carefully down for you
and cast up from your childhood,
cast up from your one hundred favorite aggies.

She has always been there, my darling.
She is, in fact, exquisite.
Fireworks in the dull middle of February
and as real as a cast-iron pot.

Let's face it, I have been momentary.
A luxury.   A bright red sloop in the harbor.
My hair rising like smoke from the car window.
Little neck clams out of season.

She is more than that.   She is your have to have,
has grown you your practical your tropical growth.
This is not an experiment.   She is all harmony.
She sees to oars and oarlocks for the dinghy,

has placed wild flowers at the window at breakfast,
sat by the potter's wheel at midday,
set forth three children under the moon,
three cherubs drawn by Michelangelo,

done this with her legs spread out
in the terrible months in the chapel.

If you glance up, the children are there
like delicate balloons resting on the ceiling.

She has also carried each one down the hall
after supper, their heads privately bent,
two legs protesting, person to person,
her face flushed with a song and their little sleep.

I give you back your heart.
I give you permission—

for the fuse inside her, throbbing
angrily in the dirt, for the bitch in her
and the burying of her wound—
for the burying of her small red wound alive—

for the pale flickering flare under her ribs,
for the drunken sailor who waits in her left pulse,
for the mother's knee, for the stockings,
for the garter belt, for the call—

the curious call
when you will burrow in arms and breasts
and tug at the orange ribbon in her hair
and answer the call, the curious call.

She is so naked and singular
She is the sum of yourself and your dream.
Climb her like a monument, step after step.
She is solid.

As for me, I am a watercolor.
I wash off.

Another of Anne Sexton's poems I wish we could read
entire is "Pain for a Daughter," which describes the mother's
anguish over a teenage daughter who has limped home,
"blind with pain," after a thoroughbred horse has stood on
her foot, leaving "the marks of the horseshoe printed/into her
flesh, the tips of her toes/ripped off like pieces of leather/three
toenails swirled like shells/and left to float in blood in her
riding boot." As the father treats her, the girl, biting on a
towel, cries out "Oh, my God help me!"

Where a child would have cried Mama!

Where a child would have believed Mama!
She bit the towel and called on God,
and I saw her life stretch out . . .
I saw her torn in childbirth,
And I saw her, at that moment,
in her own death, and I knew that she knew.

Theodore Roethke should have lived to read that poem.

In "Cinderella", one of Anne Sexton's transformations of old fairy tales, the insight is not tragic but satiric, another reappraisal of clichés about marriage, this time more unsparing than "For My Lover Returning to His Wife":

Cinderella and the prince
lived, they say, happily ever after,
like two dolls in a museum case
never bothered by diapers or dust,
never arguing over the timing of an egg,
never telling the same story twice,
never getting a middle-aged spread,
their darling smiles pasted on for eternity.
Regular Bobbsey Twins.
That story.

For Black women the problem of being a woman is compounded by race as well as sex. Life for Black women is an even more desperate daily struggle to find out what is real in their existence: how to give comfort to their men who by definition were denied their manhood for so many generations and who still find themselves in alien territory the moment they step outside their door. The idea that "Black is beautiful" has built pride and solidarity but the individual in his existential encounter with everything "out there" is no less vulnerable. In "The Alarm Clock" Mari Evans describes her shock:

Alarm clock
sure sound
loud
this mornin'

remind me of the time
I sat down

in a drug store
with my mind
a way far off

until the girl
and she was small
it seems to me
with yellow hair
a hangin'
smiled up and said
'I'm sorry but
we don't serve you people
here'
and I woke up
quick
like I did this mornin'
when the
alarm went off

It don't do
to wake up
quick

We would have no difficulty reading multiple meanings in that awakening. Miss Evans vents her anger and at the same time celebrates her pride in being a Black woman in "Vive Noir!" which moves like flood and fire across the American landscape as she vindicates her blackness:

. . . . I'm tired
of hand me downs
shut me ups
pin me ins
keep me outs
messing me over have
just had it
baby
from
you . . .

i'm
gonna spread out

over America
intrude
my proud blackness
all over the place . . . .
                    I'm
gonna make it a
    crime
        to be anything BUT black . . . .

Making love must be the world's most existential act, in
which if anywhere we grasp existence in the act itself, in which
whatever truth is realized is a private truth, a poignant
demonstration and reminder of our oneness and of the continuing paradox of the loneliness at the heart of union, the
Keatsean mystery of melancholy sitting in the very temple of
joy. Denise Levertov for whom "life is an honest breath/taken
in good faith," describes the joy and the pain in "The Ache of
Marriage":

The ache of marriage:

Thigh and tongue, beloved,
are heavy with it,
it throbs in the teeth

We look for communion
and are turned away, beloved,
each and each

It is leviathan and we
in its belly
looking for joy, some joy
not to be known outside it

two by two in the ark of
the ache of it.

Life, such poems keep saying over and over again, is experience, not a rational construct. For some the experience can
be destructive, for others a celebration. One young San
Francisco poet went on trial for poems too frank and explicit,
but she was glad to "stand witness," as she put it, "for the

divine animal and the possibility of the ecstatic access of enlightenment. My favorite word," she said, "is 'Yes'!"[12]

Adrienne Rich, too, believes in the truth of the body; intellectual life is only a half life: the emotions must be reasserted:

> Sex, as they harshly call it,
> I fell into this morning
> at ten o'clock, a drizzling hour
> of traffic and wet newspapers.

That could be a setting by Eliot, but hardly his tone as we proceed:

> I thought of him who yesterday
> clearly didn't
> turn me to a hot field
> ready for plowing,
> and longing for that young man
> pierced me to the roots
> bathing every vein, etc.
> All day he appears to me
> touchingly desirable,
> a prize one could wreck one's peace for.
> I'd call it love if love
> didn't take so many years
> but lust too is a jewel
> a sweet flower and what
> pure happiness to know
> all our high-toned questions
> breed in a lively animal.

That closes the gap the existentialists insist must be closed between the so-called higher faculties and the lower ones, the instinctive life not to be thwarted by the snobberies of the intellect, their value indeed interdependent and mutually vitalizing. Black women, loving their Black men, have never been bothered by the question at all: their existentialism could take the form "I *love*; therefore I *am*." Nikki Giovanni, given more to political activism than existential *angst*, nevertheless takes time out in a delightful piece of self satire: in "Seduction" she describes her lover's response: she has been undressing herself *and* him while he, preoccupied, talks revolution. Down to his shorts, he suddenly realizes what is going on: "Nikki," he chides, "isn't this counter-revolutionary?"

> "Black love is
> Black wealth," she says in another poem,
>
>   and they'll
> probably talk about my hard childhood
> and never understand that
> all the while I was quite happy.

Our women poets write poems not only about being a woman, in or out of the house, in or out of bed, but also about being a woman in or out of poetry. Adrienne Rich pays Emily Dickinson tribute:

> you, woman, masculine
> in single mindedness,
> for whom the word was more
> than a symptom—
>
> a condition of being.

We catch further glimpses of her descendants, Sylvia Plath and Anne Sexton and Adrienne Rich among them, for whom the word is also "a condition of being." Plath and Sexton made it their total condition: they made it half way back from bedlam, but not from death, an event already experienced in the word. Successful in refusing to sacrifice their talent, as so many women for centuries and in most cultures have had to, they ironically became a sacrifice to the talent itself, a savage god. No impositions of society, no role as mother or as wife, were more imperious than the demands of the poetry itself. But on their harrowed way to suicide they wrote brilliantly about their art. Plath's "Ariel" describes in the rhythms of horse and rider moving toward sunrise her creative drive: "I/Am the arrow,/The dew that flies/Suicidal, at one with the drive/Into the red/Eye, the cauldron of morning."

"My business is words," says Anne Sexton in "Said the Poet to the Analyst":

> I confess I am only broken by the sources of things;
> as if words were counted like dead bees in the attic,
> unbuckled from their yellow eyes and their dry wings.
> I must always forget how one word is able to pick
> out another, to manner another, until I have got
> something I might have said . . .
> but did not.

"*Your* business," she tells her analyst, "is watching my words. But I/admit nothing." "A woman who writes feels too much," she says in "The Black Art." "A man who writes knows too much."

In "Pro Femina," from which I have already quoted several passages, Carolyn Kizer is less desperate, more humorous:

> I will speak about women of letters, for I'm in the racket.

and she irreverently proceeds to review a history of women as writers, including

> . . .The married spinsters
> On loan to husbands they treated like surrogate fathers.

and

> The sad sonneteers, toast-and-teasdales we loved at
>   thirteen;
> Middle-aged virgins seducing the puerile anthologists
> Through lust-of-the-mind . . .

and

>   the Quarterly priestesses
> Who flog men for fun, and kick the women to maim
>   competition.

But, she says,

> . . .if we struggle abnormally, we may almost seem
>   normal . . .
> If we submerge our self-pity in disciplined industry;
> If we stand up and be hated, and swear not to sleep
>   with editors;
> . . .
> Keeping our heads and our pride while remaining
>   unmarried;

And if wedded, kill guilt in its tracks when we stack up
    the dishes
And defect to the typewriter.   And if mothers, believe in
    the luck of our children,
Whom we forbid to devour us, whom we shall not devour,
And the luck of our husbands and lovers, who keep
    free women.

That's a comic testament and manifesto, somewhat out of place in the company of existentialists, who prefer more fear and trembling and sickness unto death, but it is existential in its embrace of freedom, its risks and responsibilities, and in its sense of how precarious and contingent the whole enterprise is: "believe in the luck."

The confessional women poets, having made their private lives a public issue, seem less inclined to tackle grievances outside themselves, the wider world of war and social justice and the ecological threats to the green globe itself, the world that used to be considered a man's world but which men have made a mess of. It takes an ideology, a program, a movement to block nuclear proliferation or push an Equal Rights Amendment, all mechanisms important to the corporate body but anathema to the authentic life existentialism advocates. The ineluctable self shimmers at deeper levels. Yet women poets no less than their male counterparts feel the urgencies of the times and often succeed in resonating these urgencies at existential depths. "I wanted," says Nikki Giovanni, "to write

a poem
that rhymes
but revolution doesn't lead
itself to be-bopping
. . . .
perhaps these are not poetic
times
at all"

Nothing could be more contingent, more despairingly existential than certain aspects of Black life in the ghettos of America's urban jungles—Harlem or Chicago or Detroit.

Gwendolyn Brooks gives us the short happy life of a gang of Black boys in Chicago. The Pool Players Seven at the Golden Shovel:

> We real cool. We
> Left school. We
>
> Lurk late. We
> Strike straight. We
> Sing sin. We
> Thin gin. We
>
> Jazz June. We
> Die soon.

I shall let Margaret Atwood, a Canadian writer, represent the women who do anguish over the larger scene and make powerful poetry by internalizing current events, the events of their lifetimes. Here is her poem "It is Dangerous to Read Newspapers":

> While I was building neat
> castles in the sandbox,
> the hasty pits were
> filling with bulldozed corpses
>
> and as I walked to the school
> washed and combed, my feet
> stepping on the cracks in the cement
> detonated red bombs.
>
> Now I am grownup
> and literate, and I sit in my chair
> as quietly as a fuse
>
> and the jungles are flaming, the under-
> brush is charged with soldiers,
> the names on the difficult
> maps go up in smoke.
>
> I am the cause, I am a stockpile of chemical
> toys, my body
> is a deadly gadget,
> I reach out in love, my hands are guns,

my good intentions are completely lethal.

Even my
passive eyes transmute
everything I look at to the pocked
black and white of a war photo,
how
can I stop myself

It is dangerous to read newspapers.

Each time I hit a key
on my electric typewriter,
speaking of peaceful trees

another village explodes.

I promised you, by title, only glimpses of the existential strain in American women poets. I have established no existential school, no coterie, no circle or movement except to note they share an anxiety of influence—the fear they might write like a man. I have confined my sampling to the individual voices of this generation, with frequent reverberations of Emily Dickinson. Yet these vioces together do constitute a community, the kind of community that aloneness creates, the consciousness of our solitariness uniting us with the solitariness of humankind everywhere. That is the existential thing. The American woman poet, already alone and hard beset, has made a brave choice. She does not leave Eden hand in hand with Adam, as at the end of Milton's *Paradise Lost*, where, "with wandering steps and slow,/ . . . [they] took their solitarie way." Adam has kept her in his cage too long and has too often betrayed her bed and her dreams. She will go it alone, an existential decision, "where to choose/*Her* place of rest," without Milton's Providence as guide but with a great deal of self-confidence that she can work out nothing as large and abstract as her salvation but only the woman-writer-mother-wife tangle as best she can. With Emily Dickinson she can say: "I dwell in possibility." That to me sounds existential.

NOTES

1. In Barbara Segnitz and Carol Rainey, eds., *Psyche: The Feminine Poetic Consciousness. An Anthology of Modern American Women Poets* (New York: The Dial Press, 1973), p. 57. Unless otherwise indicated, passages of poetry quoted hereafter are taken from this collection.
2. Karl Malkoff, *Handbook of Contemporary American Poetry* (New York: Crowell, 1973), p. 43.
3. Quoted in K. Guru Dutt, *Existentialism and Indian Thought* (New York: Philosophical Library, 1960), p. 43.
4. From Muriel Rokeyser, "The Poem as Mask," in Florence Howe and Ellen Bass, eds., *No More Masks: An Anthology of Poems by Women* (New York: Doubleday Anchor, 1973). p. 1.
5. Recounted by Cynthia Ozick, "Women and Creativity: The Demise of the Dancing Dog," in Vivian Gornick and Barbara K. Moran, *Woman in Sexist Society* (New York: Basic Books, 1971), p. 310.
6. Vivian Gornick, "Woman as Outsider," in Gornick and Moran, p. 83.
7. "Pro Femina," in Segnitz and Rainey, p. 131.
8. Quoted in S. Laxmana Murthy, "Bakha: An Existential Analysis," *Kakatiya Journal of English Studies* (Warangal: Kakatiya University), II, 1 (Spring, 1977), p. 166.
9. Hazel Barnes, quoted in Murthy, p. 167.
10. Ibid.
11. From "The Poetry of Louise Bogan," *On the Poet and His Craft* (Seattle: Univ. of Washington, 1965), pp. 133-34.
12. Lenore Kandel, in Laura Chester and Sharon Barbara, eds., *Rising Tides: 20th Century American Women Poets* (New York: Washington Square Press, 1973), p. 218.

4

SYLVIA PLATH:
A SELF IN 'HALFLIGHTED CASTLES'

Sukrita Paul Kumar

IN a letter to Anne Sexton, Saul Bellow's message from *Herzog* said, 'Don't cry you idiot, live or die, but don't poison everything.' A kindred spirit—that of Sylvia Plath's—could also have done with a similar suggestion. Sylvia Plath's 'blood-jet of poetry' that is demonstrative of a total corpus of experience, remains, however, in the confines of tragically isolated existence. She wants to live or die, and does not take long to discover that survival is murderous and that knowing life is really knowing death. The man in the poem 'The Man at the Egg Rock' gets ready to walk into the water while his "blood (is) beating the old tattoo/I am, I am, I am". He makes this existential declaration as he determines to drown himself. Sylvia's "I am", too, sought to realize itself only through a direct confrontation with death.

In an autobiographical essay, "Ocean 1212-W", which gets its title from Sylvia's grandparents' phone number, she describes how when she was two-and-a-half years old, on the day her brother was born, she walked along the beach and saw for the first time "the separateness of everything". This was as she says "the awful birthday of otherness": "I felt the wall of my skin: I am I. That stone is a stone". It is interesting to see her in a reverse situation in 'Poem for a Birthday', when having been through a mental illness, she identifies herself with inanimate objects: "I am a root, a stone, an owl pellet/without dreams of any sort". Significantly, this loss of complete identity is followed by remorse and anger: "Mother of otherness/Eat me". In the third part of the same poem, "Maenad", she is conscious of assuming a new self, an identity different from the earlier—"I am becoming *another*". She asserts herself rather negatively—"Tell me my name". This I think is a valuable clue to the understanding of the dynamic emerging of a poetic identity, the agonising oscillations of Sylvia's spirit between birth and rebirth, annihilation and reconstruction of her soul between life and death. Joyce Carol Oates comments perceptively over the 'I' of Sylvia Plath's poetry. The dramatic persona, she says, is an artful construction, a tragic figure whose tragedy is classical, the result of a limited vision that believed itself to be the mirror held up to nature as in the poem "Mirror": "I am not cruel, only truthful/the eye of a little god". This, she says, is the audacious *hubris* of tragedy, the inevitable reality-challenging statement of the participant in a dramaic action he does not know is tragic. The drama of Sylvia Plath's self enacted in her poetry is in fact a pointed revelation of the "outsider-spirit" of the artist testing reality.[1] Colin Wilson's existentialist in *The Outsider* declares "I am God". So does Sylvia Plath in the "Mirror". Only, this awareness, the heightened perception also encompasses in its range of experience, a petrifying hurt which sharpens with spiritual growth and maturity: "We grow/It hurts at first. The red tongues will teach the truth" ("Poem for a Birthday"), "I am lost, I am lost, in the robes of all this light". In "Three Women" the poet announces in anguish, "I am solitary as grass. What is it I miss?/Shall I ever find it, whatever it is?" The restless quest and the associated feeling of solitariness, of "lackness" and of a nauseating alertness of "being" are projected in verses charged with an insatiable urge to live: "Drunk as a foetus/I suck at the paps of darkness" ("Poem for a Birthday"). What does recovery from the mental illness bring for her—daylight which "lays its sameness on the wall" and the realization that "Down there one is alone" ("Blue Moles").

Sylvia associates the curative process with love; but love is an ambiguous force which can combine both affection and menace: "Love is the uniform of my bald nurse./Love is the bone and sinew of my curse" ("Poem for a Birthday"). She regards the therapeutic value of love, of "togetherness" rather suspiciously and cynically. She imagines herself as filled with emptiness, as a wound "walking out of hospital". For her, therefore, attachment "with the other" or the pronouncements of a practical-minded, combative, "healthy" society of organized individuals are meaningless. Her body is a "vase reconstructed" that houses "the elusive rose". The Outsider is not sure he *is*. Sylvia Plath locates an elusive "I" which may not be the true "I". The journey begins once again and dislocated "I" has to find its way back home. The question of identity, like a pendulum, moves as a prisoner in halflighted castles, from one shadow to another. During this indefatigable process there are pauses when the Snakecharmer "tires of music/and pipes the world back to the simple fabric/ of snake-warp, snake-weft . . . (he) Puts up his pipe, and lids his moony eye" ("Snakecharmer"). Sylvia herself is a "snakecharmer" who constructs a world of her own with her perception; and, when tired, reclines in the solitary ego of her own self, a prison. Her own children are objects of her perception. They are, with the rest of the world, under her scrutiny and fall into the fabric of creativity in whatever design or image she selects. Her "will to power", her greed for more life and her vividness of sense-perception separate her from the rest. And, it is the consciousness of separateness that is the cause of her anguished self and she meditates: "It is the exceptional that interests the devil./I do not will (my baby) to be exceptional/. . . . . I will him to be common" ("Three Women"). She is herself an "exception" and what alienation torments her should not be inflicted on her baby.

In her poem "Black Rook in Rainy Weather" Sylvia Plath celebrates an experience which would offer itself only to the rare "exceptions", the selected few human beings. She perceives a miracle and says, "I only know that a rook/ordering its black feathers can so shine/As to seize my senses, haul/My eyelids up, and grant/A brief respite from the fear of total neutrality". That "rare, random descent" of the angel exhilirated the life-force of the artist. She escaped the triviality and mundanity of existence during such radiant miracles that rendered new dimensions to her self. Each such exalted experience would further whet her appetite for more; and with the end, her wait for another would begin again. In her poem "Mystic", she says "The heart has not stopped . . ./Once one has seen God, What is the remedy?"

Her "parenthetical" existence is slashed with a wishful encounter with death when the knife would enter "Pure and clean as the cry of a baby,/And the universe slide from my side". An identification of her own self with the self of the Queen-bee in the poem, "Stings", presents the question of the recovery of the self after a death: "They thought death was worth it, but I/Have a self to recover, a queen". Throughout her life Sylvia struggled to gather the scattered selves of her personality trying to conjoin as she says "myself" with "myself" ("The Other"). The disintegrated personality, in medical terms the schizo-phrenic self, is herself conscious of her broken soul: "The glass cracks across,/The image/Flees and aborts like dropped mercury" ("Thalidomide"). The consciousness hovering in the charged area between herself and herself looks in both the directions: it is magnetically pulled by the affirmative conjoin-ing, the "pure" sought in death, and the negative pole, "deferr-ing to reality", a plaster saint of a self—stiff and spinsterish—building a barricade of "barb and check/Against mutinous weather/As no more insurgent man could hope to break/With curse, fist, threat/Or love, either" ("Spinster"). Her world becomes a world of alienations—man from man, man from nature, man from God. So much so that the distance between the opposed selves of the same personality, too, becomes immeasurable. Her poems revolve in the rhythms and images of "breakdown" and "breakthrough". Everything is a trap, a prison, a hook or a bell-jar. Even her own children and her husband present "hooks in their smiles" from which she hangs precariously.

Concrete images of annihilation in the "Colossus" as well as the "Ariel" poems record processes of depletion of the poet's own self. With a sharp awareness of sublunar darkness, what she seeks is a stance and a collection of selves. Her poetry is a poetry of anticipation of perfection, of death. Dying, as we know, is an art according to Sylvia. There is an interplay of destruction and creation, and there is a harmony through diffusion. The highly modern sensibility of the poet is ridden with guilt and suffering. She dies repeatedly, poem after poem exorcizing her self from all prejudices, guilts and pangs through confessions. Impersonalizing her selves into poetry and repeatedly talking about "fixity", "perfection" and "death", she combines the three in the pcem "Medallion". "Perfection", she said, "is terrible, it cannot have children". The fluidity that is witnessed in her earlier poems gradually moves to a motionless stasis. In her last poem "Edge", Sylvia Plath gives birth to her vision of the final reality. The poetic persona of this poem enfolds herself as well as her children into a "separate garden"—a sealed prison. "The other" is done away with and it is one unique self that becomes the subject/object of this self-created world which is merged into the "impersonal" through "death". The self demonstrates a direct Nietzschean drive for control, erects a deity of "self" with a very masculine will to power.

Gordon Lameyer who had an affair with Sylvia talks about Sylvia's "narcissism" and her masochistically self-inflicted self-induced suffering, and accuses her of ego-centrism.[2] On the other hand Dorothea Krook in her recollections of Sylvia Plath says, "Sylvia was extraordinarily modest, self-effacing, unassuming, unspoilt; never inviting attention to herself, seeming to want only the selfless intellectual relationship."[3] The duality of her self projects itself, as mentioned earlier, in her poetry, too. And, her sense of "being", it appears, acquires a complexity and ambiguity precisely because she is a "woman". It should be a worthwhile study to explore the range of her experience as a woman and the consequent perspective and the positioning of her self in her family, in society and in the universe.

The Bell Jar is praised by some critics as a chronicle of "genuinely feminist aspirations", and Germaine Greer has claimed that if a few feminists had been around in 1963, Sylvia Plath would not have had to commit suicide. This is obviously a prejudiced and restrictive understanding of Sylvia Plath's self. Though there is no denying the fact that much of her poetry is conspicuously born out of a woman's experience: there are poems about pregnancy, giving birth, or the relationship of the mother with the infant ("Magi", "Love Letter", "Candles", "Metaphors" etc.); also, there are poems which demonstrate the daughter/father relationship, the

person of a spinster, a widow, the relationship with other
women and men as well as children, etc. There is a concrete,
powerful stock of imagery from feminine sources in the
poems . . . of the child's nursery, keeping the kitchen and
houshold objects.

Sylvia Plath suffers a curious, well-known childhood
fixation for her father, which best comes out in the parricidal
poem "Daddy". Her relationship and approach to other men
are rather warped despite her assertion, "Daddy, Daddy, you
bastard, I'm through". She is *not* through and she remains
the victim as well as the victimizer. She is conscious of
the deepest guilt of her own split personality and the destructive forces within her own self. Her kinship with her mother
smacks of a sense of violent unease. And there is a marked
hostility towards other women. In the poem "Lesbos" she
expresses her personal antipathy for them: "Every woman's a
whore./I can't communicate". "Lesbos", it seems, is a very
concentrated statement about the false, hypocritical relationship between the so-called enlightened young mothers in the
world of modern apartment complex. The transcendence of
this ordinary self is effectively voiced in "Fever 103" when the
self enters a pure, deathless realm:

> "I think I am going up,
> I think I may rise—
> The beads of hot metal fly, and I, love, I
> Am a pure acetylene
> Virgin
> Attended by roses . . . .
> (My selves dissolving, old whore petticoats)
> To Paradise."

Her selves are "old, petticoats" and she seeks a liberation
from them in "Winter Trees". She displays an identification
with trees and envies them their freedom from the woman's
fate of "copulation, abortion and bitchery". Essentially,
therefore, what her self demands is a total surrender of being,
or perhaps a triumph in death, in impersonality. A "Lady
Lazarus", she rejects the theatrical for the real and says:
"Dying/Is an art, like everything else./I do it exceptionally

well./I do it so it feels like hell/I do it so it feels *real*." The poem, "Lady Lazarus", is also an act of revenge on the male ego: "Out of the ash/I rise with my red hair/And I eat men like air".

It is a rare experience to meet Sylvia Plath while she is "learning Peacefulness" as in the poem, "Tulips", which to my mind, is one of her masterpieces of craftsmanship. She celebrates in this, her self-effacement ("I am nobody") when she has given her name and clothes, marks of identification, to the nurse, and, has parted with her history to the anaes-thetist and has given her body to the surgeon. She continues, "I am a nun now, I have never been so pure". Unattached, empty and unawre of her own ego, and freed from the narcissus, she rejoices in her freedom and peacefulness. "I smile, a budha, . . . ask nothing of life" ("Paralytic")—This is what she craves for—a selflessness.

Sylvia Plath's alignment with the universe in the poem "The Night Dances", makes her aware of the comets and the space they have to cross. The coldness and forgetfulness that is associated with them, are, in fact, symptomatic of the total lack of communication and the "cold folds of her own ego" she suffers. The night dances; so also does the psyche of the persona of the poem, a universe in itself. The utter lone-liness of herself and of her petrified will seeks to express itself through poetry, the creation of which is in it self a process of self-realization.

Sylvia Plath underwent four months' psychoanalysis at Mclean before completing her Honour's thesis at Smith. It was George Gibion's course on Dostoevsky that gave her deep insights into the use of "doubles" in his fiction. The formal psychoanalysis at Mclean did not help her as much in the understanding of her own nervous disorders, attempted suicide and recovery, as Dostoevsky's structure of the "doubles". In fact, her Honour's thesis, *The Magic Mirror* (1955), is an analysis of the dynamics of "the double" in Dostoevsky, the technique used to project the schizophrenic fears upon either a hallucinatory figure or another human being. Many poems by Sylvia Plath contain references to mirrors and to "doubles" which are psychological projections of some aspect of the speaker. Most of all, she explored the psychological double in her semi-autobiographical novel, *The Bell Jar*. Otto Rank the psychoanalyst relates narcissism with the creation of the double. It is the narcissist's failure, he says, to fulfill love needs in childhood that causes the personality to split, projecting onto another the deepest guilts and destructive forces within the self. The anguish of the schizophrenic heroine of *The Bell Jar*, Esther Greenwood, is uncovered with poetic intensity and somewhere between the heroine's doubles is Sylvia Plath's own shadow emerging in different shades of black and white. Like Sylvia Plath Esther is unconsciously facing the dilemma of whether to allow herself to become more divided and finally shatter into madness or to get well. Playing with the ball of silver mercury she says, "If I dropped it, it would break into a million little replicas of itself, and if I pushed them near each other, they would fuse without a crack, into one whole again." The polarized selves of her personality yield intense conflict and she is like the "train" dragging herself, screaming: "an animal/ Insane for the destination,/ The bloodspot/ The face at the end of the flare" ("The Train").

Instead of making her soar high in release, the hallucinatory projectings of her self reduce her ego to a numbness. She is alerted about the "bell-jar" under which her "self" dissolves: "See, the darkness is leaking from the cracks./ I cannot contain it. I cannot contain my life."

Though Ted Hughes describes the births of the two children as crucial stages in his wife's movement toward self-acceptance, this very reality of the two children, we know, also, presented "hooks" to her. And, as in "A Birthday Present", death approaches her with a promise when "split lives (will) congeal and stiffen to history".

"Creation", they say, "is the great mime, and creating is living doubly." Sylvia not only lived doubly, she also died doubly. With all her intensified sense of life, she knows that the interpretation of existence depends on our experience of death. Death in her case is a spiritual self-affirmation.

NOTES

1. Joyce Carol Oates, "The Death Throes of Romanticism: The Poetry of Sylvia Plath", Essay in Edward Butsher ed., *Sylvia Plath*: *The Woman and the Work* (New York : Dodd, Mead & Co., 1977) pp. 206-224.
2. "Sylvia at Smith", in Butsher ed., *Sylvia Plath*, pp. 32-42.
3. "Recollections of Sylvia Plath," in Butsher ed., *Sylvia Plath*, pp. 49-60.

5

EXISTENTIALIST APPROACH TO MODERN AMERICAN DRAMA

Ruby Chatterji

EXISTENTIALISM as a philosophic stance is by origin a Continental phenomenon. Two nineteenth century thinkers, Kierkegaard, a Dane, and Nietzsche, a German, are recognised as initiators of the movement, particularly in their concept of the individual existent, as also in their diagnosis of the modern human predicament. While Kierkegaard may be regarded as the Protestant of Protestants, Nietzsche, having pronounced the death of God, takes his position as an atheist, and this radical division has prevailed between Christian and humanistic existentialists: to place for example Jaspers and Marcel on one side and Sartre and Camus on the other, though Heidegger claimed to be neither theist nor atheist. What they none the less share in common as existentialists is their concept of *man-in-this-world*. They view the individual as existing in his subjective concreteness and the self as a dynamic agent involved in a situation of inevitable tension and conflict. They see the existent individual as usually confronted with the norms of bourgeois society, the authoritarian state, abstract philosophical theories, static systems, objective scientific knowledge and modern technological civilization.

Both in their philosophic and literary writings existentialists have sought to define precisely the various subjective states of this actual and concrete individual being. Camus passionately evokes the moment when an individual discovers for himself a lack of purpose and meaning in his habitual way of life. The entire human condition—including metaphysical reality, nature, society, the civilized structures of logic and language—strikes him as 'absurd'. He can only assert the bare fact that he exists and protest that he feels totally alienated both from himself and things other than himself. Camus finally sees the consciousness of the absurd as a kind of liberation for the individual who can then exercise his freedom by a metaphysical revolt. Sartre takes a more positive view in formulating his idea of 'existence before essence'. He denies man any given essence or abstract human nature and advocates the recognition of 'anxiety' and 'absurdity' as necessary prerequisities to the definition of self through a series of conscious and irrevocable choices. While most existentialists follow Kierkegaard and Heidegger in emphasizing a moment of authenticity when an absolute either/or decision is taken, Sartre extends it by insisting that the individual must face the anguish of conscious decision at every instant of his life, since he is burdened with the terrible freedom and responsibility to make or create himself. Sartre also asserts that although there is no universal human nature there is a universal human condition. When the absurdity of life is fully recognized, the dread converted, the choice made and the responsibilty assumed, existence is felt as a value in itself. Existentialism thus becomes an active way of life to be practised and lived through effort and achievement.

Since existentialism deals with problems related to concrete human existence, existentialist thinkers have often found their best mode of expression in imaginative literature: in drama, fiction, creative prose and poetry. This would apply to philosophers like Sartre and Camus as well as to writers like Dostoevsky, Kafka, Rilke, Durrenmatt and such others who reveal the existentialist sensibility mainly in their literary works. In post-war Europe an entire dramatic movement, later labelled 'the theatre of the absurd,' emerged primarily as a consequence of the existentialist double-focus on absurd-man-in-an-absurd-human-condition. It covers such widely different dramatists as Beckett, Ionesco, Adamov, Genet and Pinter. Existentialist literature tends to emphasize certain recurring themes: man alienated from an absurd world; the individual estranged from society; the individual's isolation and subjectivity; his consequent feelings of anxiety, anguish, despair, nausea; the individual facing his own nothingness, or confronting his guilt; his struggle to distinguish between inauthentic and authentic selves; his assertion of personal freedom through irrevocable choice, particularly in extreme situations, limit situations and crisis situations; death consciousness and the need to define oneself against it; the victim-hero who creates his own values from within. As a literary phenomenon its distinctiveness lies in the philosophically specialized form of its quest for authentic selfhood and analysis of the human condition, which acquire psychological subtlety, metaphysical intensity and a sense of emotional urgency that are peculiarly modern. In short, it is a kind of literature that has the ability to convey the sense of a crisis in civilization. That two world wars and their aftermath, together with the rise of the totalitarian state, should give birth to such a complex of philosophic thought and feeling in Western Europe is both explicable and not unexpected. Yet, existentialist literature has had far wider repurcussions, and might be traced as a world-wide phenomenon by the mid-twentieth century. It has even been maintained that the existentialist sensibility, as distinguished from existentialism as a modern European movement, crosses both historical and geographical boundaries. At the same time, perhaps, some caution is necessary in the use of the term, particularly in a literary context.

Sartre once expressed his disapproval of the common tendency to apply the term 'existentialist' so loosely and imprecisely as to render it practically useless.[1] Where American drama is concerned critics have behaved in a rather cavalier fashion by bringing under the existentialist umbrella plays which have only a tenuous link with genuine existentialist themes and attitudes. For example, Elmer Rice's *The Adding Machine* (1923), which should properly be characterized as 'expressionistic', has often been listed under existentialist drama.[2] It must be understood that the presence of vaguely similar ideas or motifs does not warrant a leap to the conclusion that the play is wholly or even partially existentialist. With the exception of Eugene O'Neill, what seems basically lacking in modern American drama is that ultimate metaphysical dimension without which no imaginative work can be

categorized as truly existentialist. Themes such as consciousness of the absurd, revolt, choice and authenticity, in the
existentialist sense, must finally transcend all social and
psychological cause-and-effect relationships, even while paradoxically embracing concrete experience.

Of the older generation of American dramatists, it is
Eugene O'Neill, who, particularly in his last phase, attained
that metaphysical anguish which is the central existentialist
experience. *The Iceman Cometh* (1939) can be seen as perhaps
the most existentialist of O'Neill's plays, as also his most
mature. O'Neill was fully aware of its metaphysical dimension, since he had himself commented: "*The Iceman* is a denial
of any other experience of faith in my plays."[3] Here, in a
Nietzschean Godless world, O'Neill is probing deeply into the
fundamental nature of human existence focusing on the role of
illusions in life. Though his conclusions might seem to differ,
O'Neill is in fact grappling with some of the major existentialist themes, such as self-deception and authenticity, problems
which exercised both Sartre and Heidegger. O'Neill's preoccupation with death—as the final limit set to human
existence, as well as the inevitable end towards which all life
seems to proceed—is not unlike the death-consciousness of
existentialist thinkers. Heidegger cryptically defined death as
"the possibility of the impossibility of any existence at all,"[4]
and urged that this fact be constantly embraced in all decision
making as the existent's inward awareness that his being is a
"being-towards-death".

The setting of *The Iceman* is Harry Hope's saloon, a dirty
and dingy place, significantly and symbolically described
as "the No Choice Saloon, Bedrock Bar, The End of the Line
Cafe, The Bottom of the Sea Rathskeller", "where no one has
to worry about where they are going next". Here, a group of
drunken derelicts share a claustrophobic existence drowning
themselves in drink. These figures, all drop-outs from the
normal society outside, are types drawn from different walks
of life who together represent alienated humanity in a predicament of near-despair. Similar types and similar situations
have commonly found favour with existentialist writers for the
purpose of exploring extreme states of mind in extreme
conditions.

What is interesting to observe, however, is how through mutual tolerance and understanding these down-and-outs have formed themselves into a kind of 'alternative society,' composed of small units of close and interdependent relationships, in groups of two and three. The settlement is complete with Hope as their benefactor and protector, Jimmy as their leader of the 'To-morrow Movement', and Larry as the supposedly detached philosopher.

In the characteristic existentialist manner the play's focus is on the states of consciousness of this derelict group. Though Hope's alchohol has reduced them to a condition of drunken somnolence—some even keep passing out from time to time— yet they cling on tenaciously to their favourite 'pipe-dreams', their illusions about yesterdays and to-morrows. Befitting the character types, there is a wide range of these pipe-dreams which project different forms of social integration and social success, all to be achieved 'to-morrrow', a day of action that can always be safely postponed. The concomitant tendency to sentimentalize over illusory past events and incidents is simultaneously present. In spite of the fact that the inmates seem aware of the hollowness of one another's pipe-dreams, which become the targets of ironical banter, in each case the individual illusion is allowed to persist. The pipe-dreams must be viewed as the last hope which keeps the derelicts going. These figures are thus shown by O'Neill as both estranged from society and alienated from themselves. The reflection is on the human condition in general, though it also entails an indirect indictment of the particular social myths and images people are expected to live up to in the modern world.

One prospect the group shares in common is the coming of Hickey, the travelling salesman, in time for Hope's birthday party, when the booze will flow freely and the 'gang' entertained to Hickey's broad jokes about his loving wife and the iceman. This event appears to be an annual ritual almost signifying a mystical renewal of life for the group. At the opening, the derelicts are seen to eagerly expect and impatiently await Hickey's arrival, but the developing action of the play existentially and ironically brings about the tragic shattering of this group illusion, as well as of the individual pipe-dreams, when Hickey actually comes.

Against this close group of dimly conscious drunkards, three characters stand out as more complexly realized individuals, who form a triangle of tension and conflict as the play progresses. Larry, the 'grandstand philosopher', lives with the group but assumes the role of a cynically detached observer who has shed his pipe-dreams. As the reflective *raisonneur*-commentator his position is that of an insider who ironically believes himself to be an outsider in relation to the group. Parritt, who is young, weak-willed and shifty, comes as a fugitive from the outside world to seek shelter within the group. Hickey, the hardware salesman, is the outsider who starts manipulating the group with self-confidence and bonhomie, but grows aggressive and destructive in his attempts to sell salvation. As with Sartre, O'Neill is interested in displaying different types of consciousness taking shape in relation to a given situation.

The play reveals deliberate acts of choice undertaken by these three characters which may be regarded as existentialist decisions: on account of their crucial significance in each case, the emotional intensity accompanying the choice, the crisis situations which generate them, and finally, in the way they change the entire shape of the lives of the individuals concerned. All are in some form acts of betrayal involving different degrees of self-deception, comparable to Sartre's *mauvaise foi* or 'bad faith'. The actions prove almost equally destructive, in the sense that they result not only in the deaths of their victims, but ultimately lead the performers to embrace their own deaths. The choices are also tragic, since the disturbing sense of guilt that grips the characters as a consequence of their actions brings about different kinds of self-knowledge and self-recognition, which help the characters to make their final existential resolutions of facing death.

Hickey represents perhaps O'Neill's finest example of the layers of self-deception that have to be stripped off before one can even touch one's true self. When Hickey arrives just in time for Hope's birthday, despite his heartiness and good cheer it is noticeably a changed Hickey. Hickey not only abstains from drink claiming to have found total peace and freedom, but even announces his intention to save the inmates of Hope's saloon. His uncomfortable hints set everyone on edge practically ruining the party, so that the observant Larry refers to it as 'Nihilist Hickey's Revolution'. Hickey's odd and unusual behaviour stems from his existentialist act of having killed his wife in the state of self-deception that it was good for both of them. This has led him to the further delusion that he must now save his boon companions by making them face up to the truth about themselves, as he believes he has himself done.

The brand of salvation Hickey offers them may be labelled 'Action to-day' as opposed to their 'To-morrow Movement'. After zealous persuasion when Hickey actually manages to get Hope and his group to act out their pipe-dreams the result is altogether disastrous. This confrontation of their own nothingness becomes for them as annihilating an experience as the icy touch of death. Even the booze seems to have lost its kick as if bewitched by Hickey. It is existentialist experience forced upon the reluctant inmates from outside, and therefore not perhaps altogether genuine. Within the symbolical structure of the play Hickey can be identified as the Iceman-Death, the antagonist of Hope-Life.

Witnessing the actual effect of his conversion to be the opposite of the expected peace, Hickey himself feels profoundly disturbed, which launches him on his long self-probing confessional. Hickey inadvertently admits to having killed his wife, not out of his great love for her, to stop her suffering his repeated moral lapses, as he had earlier persuaded himself, but because he had come to hate her for her blind credulousness and sweet forgiving nature. This existentialist shock of authentic self-revelation as the suppressed truth surfaces to Hickey's consciousness proves too much for him. Hickey immediately seeks refuge in another self-deception that he must have gone crazy at that point. Hope and his group foster this illusion clutching at it as their last straw. If Hickey is insane his salvation mission is equally a madman's delusion, and they can now safely revert back to their own pipe-dreams. Hickey's calling the police *prior* to his confessional monologue also indicates that his sense of peace and freedom was in 'bad faith', a mere cloak to cover up his guilt-ridden conscience.

In certain respects Parritt's case runs parallel to Hickey's, so that there is some subconscious identification with Hickey on Parritt's part, felt at first as instinctive hostility, later realized as situational affinity. Parritt has informed on his anarchist mother resulting in her imprisonment, which, as Parritt admits, for a freedom loving woman like her equates death. Though at the beginning he tries to conceal this fact, appealing to Larry's sympathy as his mother's one-time-lover and a deserter like himself, he actually wants Larry to pass judgement on him as his father-surrogate. Yet, Parritt tries to deceive Larry as to his real motives, first by the bluff of his love for the nation, next by imputing to himself the Judas role of betraying for money, deliberately to provoke Larry out of his pretended unconcern. Listening to Hickey's monologue, he responds to it point by point as though it was simultaneously his own confession. He even goes one step beyond by repudiating Hickey's subterfuge of insanity. Parritt is finally induced to acknowledge openly that it was naked hate for his dominating yet loveless mother that incited him to act as he did. In the scheme of the play this must be seen as Parritt's existentialist choice paralleling Hickey's. Prompted by Larry, Parritt's subsequent suicide marks the weak man's attempt to escape his guilt-stricken self, and thus represents the negative existential act.

Larry, the self-styled cynic, presents a more complex existentialist figure as he is also made to see through his cynic's self-deception by becoming gradually involved in the action. His spontaneous condemnation of Parritt is a full-fledged existentialist decision arrived at in great anguish of heart, one for which he assumes total responsibility. At the point of Parritt's suicide Larry feels curiously overwhelmed by a mixed feeling of guilt and pity which constitutes his moment of authenticity: "I'll never be a success at the grandstand—or anywhere else! Life is too much for me! I'll be a weak fool looking with pity at the two sides of everything till the day I die ! May that day come soon!" Larry realizes that his detachment had been as much a pose as his grandstand of welcoming death was a cover for his cowardice. His transformation from the posture of detached philosopher to the consciousness of his own absurdity as a failure compounded of cowardice and compassion, is an existententialist experience *par excellence*

which prepares him finally to accept death. This is why Larry
concludes ironically that he is the only 'convert' Hickey has
made. Within the play's social pattern he becomes totally isolated from Hope's group as he stands soliloquizing to himself,
now in the position of the real 'outsider' in Hope's alternative
society.

The existentialist mode of the play demands that death be
present on the threshold of consciousness of the characters
though the individual response to death admits variety. With
the exception of Larry who achieves a positive existentialist
position with regard to death, O'Neill reveals a series of
negative existentialist attitudes. The chilling touch of the
Iceman is soon forgotten by Hope and his group who will
drink and dream away their days waiting for the end. Despite
his double disillusion—with his wife and his boon companions—
Hickey, the lost saviour, clings pathetically to the plea of
madness, his last self-evasion, even while surrendering himself
to the law, which means the electric chair. Parritt's leap to
death is a desperate solution for his crisis of conscience, in
fact an escape.

As is the case with much existentialist literature, the problem of 'truth' constitutes the central issue of *The Iceman.* At
the beginning of the play Larry had pronounced in a mocking
cynical vein, "To hell with the truth! As the history of the
world proves, the truth has no bearing on anything. Its
irrelevant and immaterial, as the lawyers say. The lie of a
pipe-dream is what gives life to the whole misbegotten mad
lot of us, drunk or sober." The problem remains as to how
far O'Neill actually endorses this position through the action
of the play, particularly its end when Hope and his protégés
are allowed to drift back contentedly into their haven of
pipe-dreams. O'Neill is reported to have explained to an
interviewer:

The philosophy is that there is always one dream left, one
final dream, no matter how low you have fallen, down there
at the bottom of the bottle. I know, because I saw it.[5]

As a corollary to this view, the play seems to suggest

further that demolition of the last illusion equates death. Yet, a careful analysis reveals that the play's structure is more dialectical than circular. Larry's initial dismissal of truth as totally irrelevant is countered by Hickey's traditional evangelical doctrine of facing the truth about oneself. It is as though Larry plays 'jesting Pilate' to Hickey's role of modern Messiah. What the play's conclusion offers is actually a new level of paradoxical but *existentialist truth* born of action and experience. Since men are weak and limited and life appears to be meaningless in a Godless world, human beings should view one another with pity and compassion, oneself not excluded. In the human predicament illusions are a necessary truth of life and must be tolerated as such.

O'Neill's inquiry into the nature of the human condition is made in the existentialist mode, though his conclusion seems to indicate a position somewhat different from that of his Continental compeers. Heidegger and Sartre are more demanding, and perhaps relatively more optimistic, in urging authentic selfhood through the realization of that terrible freedom which is 'total responsibility in total solitude'; Camus advocates 'metaphysical rebellion' in the face of the absurdity of the universe. O'Neill appears to be more tolerant if pessimistic in emahasizing the limits of the self rather than its possibilities. In *The Iceman* Larry alone among all the characters may be said to have attained both authenticity of self and a mental state of revolt. Arguably, O'Neill can be regarded as a tragic playwright as well as an existentialist humanist in his own right. His comments on the play are sufficiently illuminating from this point of view:

> . . . there are moments in it that suddenly strip the secret soul of a man stark naked, not in cruelty or moral superiority, but with an *understanding compassion* which sees him as *a victim of the ironies of life and of himself.* Those moments are for me the depth of tragedy, with nothing more that can possibly be said.[6] (My italics.)

In his more autobiographical play, *A Long Day's Journey into Night* (1940), written, as he describes, 'in tears and blood', O'Neill puts himself in the character of Edmund, the younger

son of the cursed Tyrone family. Incorporating as it does a
wealth of personal and familial allusions, the play none the
less has universal implications and reflects upon the human
condition. O'Neill concentrates on the nightmare existence
of two generations of a bourgeois Irish-Catholic family,
propelling back in memory to a past third generation. Each
member of this family is inextricably enmeshed in a vicious
network of guilt, inadequacy, self-deception and recrimina-
tion, to which each has contributed and of which each is a
victim. At the same time, there is also love, compassion
and understanding that holds them together in spite of their
mutual damage.

O'Neill digs relentlessly into the past of these characters
in an effort to discover the source of the blight which is
devastating the family. Economic, psychological and moral
causes are offered, but the explanations never seem adequate.
James Tyrone Senior's petty-bourgeois idea of thrift plus the
self-centred pursuit of his actor's career are clearly responsible
for his wife's morphine addiction and her sense of insecurity
in not having a proper home. Edmund's tuberculosis terrifies
Mary into resumption of her drug habit, since she cannot get
away from the guilt of a neglected and lost son, or from the
fact that her father died of the same disease. Mary's fantasy
withdrawal into her convent-girl past creates the atmosphere
of inescapable helplessness which causes Jamie to despair
altogether of reforming his own debauched life. Jamie has
already frittered away his actor's talent reducing himself to a
self-deprecating 'Might-Have-Been.' Tyrone Senior, too, had
earlier betrayed his own talent by plumping for a popular
money-making role, while Mary's adolescent dream of becoming a nun or a concert pianist, had been abandoned without a
struggle. Having revealed a series of self-betrayals and other
interlinking factors leading to the family's present predicament,
O'Neill suggests additionally a kind of all-encompassing determinism which is his despairing vision of the human condition.
As Mary pronounces it, "None of us can help the things life
has done to us. They're done before you realize it, and once
they're done they make you do other things until at last
everything comes between you and what you'd like to be, and
you've lost your true self forever." In its concern for the self

as a victim of the human condition O'Neill's play already approaches existentialist thought.

More importantly, the play also projects an individual existentialist consciousness in the figure of Edmund, the surrogate for O'Neill himself. Edmund is aware that his mother's addiction is linked with his birth, and consequently his very existence seems to him accursed. His father's close-fistedness, his mother's evasion of the truth about his illness, and his own inherited weak constitution, merely enhance his sense of the meaninglessness of life. Yet, the sum of these factors would fail to account fully for Edmund's agonized quest for selfhood or his lacerating feeling of estrangement from the world. Quite symptomatically he quotes Nietzsche: "God is dead: of his pity for man hath God died." Edmund has flirted with socialism, laboured as a sailor for a pittance, and even attempted to commit suicide. "We are such stuff as manure is made on, so let's drink up and forget it": his parody of Shakespeare crystallizes his excremental vision of mankind. He desires to escape from his dreary daily existence into the night fog: "The fog was where I wanted to be . . . That's what I wanted – to be alone with myself in another world where truth is untrue and life can hide from itself . . . It felt damned peaceful to be nothing more than a ghost within a ghost." This experience of the annihilation of self is only momentarily transcended by his ecstatic experience at sea:

> I belonged without past or future, within peace and unity and a wild joy, within something greater than my own life, or the life of Man, to life itself! . . . For a second there is meaning! Then the hand lets the veil fall and you are alone, lost in the fog again, and you stumble on toward nowhere, for no good reason!

Edmund's dominating consciousness remains persistently one of existentialistic alienation: "As it is I will always be a stranger who never feels at home, who does not really want and is not really wanted, who can never belong, who must always be a little in love with death." Such feelings clearly articulate the basic existentialist motifs, and recall vividly the experience of estrangement in Camus' *The Outsider*. Having encountered the 'absurd' Edmund chooses for himself a type of revolt also advocated by Camus: he seeks to define himself by exercising the 'absurd freedom' of the artist and write poetry.

The other three Tyrones, who are also described as 'fog people', approach a quasi-existentialist sensibility in their feeling of isolation, self-contempt, and self-evasion through drug or drink. Even Jamie, despite his inverted protest of whoring and drinking, and his moment of truth when he warns his brother against himself, cannot claim to have attained a fully existentialist awareness. Unlike Edmund, these others have recourse to different escape routes into oblivion rather than face up to an absurd reality.

Among the younger generation of American dramatists, it is Edward Albee who exhibits a positive existentialist impulse, and his first one-acter, *The Zoo Story* (1959), is perhaps the most successful existentialist play in the American theatre to date. It not only integrates recognizably existentialist themes and motifs, but by symbolic extension of the local and particular, manages to evoke convincingly the universal human situation and even the necessary metaphysical dimension.

The Zoo Story treats the experience, decision and irrevocable action of Jerry, the existentialist man, who describes himself paradoxically but significantly as a "permanent transient." Jerry is seen to confront Peter, a conformist representative of the American middle-class, who has been living a complacent life with a cushy job, a comfortable home, the average number of children, and the right status symbols. Peter occupying a bench in Central Park, on a Sunday afternoon, to read his book, takes for granted that this is his own secure and private corner, his bourgeois property. Jerry, who is in many ways his opposite, has no family, and has lived in a shabby rooming house with various other social riffraff, brooding over his own rather sordid past. The kind of society and its norms which Peter embodies, and Jerry is impelled to protest against, is one that Karl Jaspers had indicted as a threat to genuine human existence.

As a social outcast, Jerry has experienced the existentialist agony of total isolation and discovered the meaninglessness of concepts such as 'sense', 'order', and 'neat categorization'. For Jerry both society and the entire human condition are as frustrating as his image of the zoo: "with everyone separated by bars from everyone else, the animals for the most part from each other and always the people from the animals." The cages are those of social convention and false values, while the animals symbolically represent different categories of human beings. Jerry is therefore intensely concerned with the fundamental human problem of making contact: with objects, with animals, with people, with ideas, and ultimately, perhaps, with God in human form.

Jerry's story of his unsuccessful effort to make a beginning with the loathsome landlady's ferocious dog becomes highly meaningful as a concrete existentialist experience. Jerry first bribed the dog with hamburgers to express his love and subsequently poisoned him to kill him, both of which failed; the dog on recovery gave him a long stare which was a point of contact, but then withdrew altogether allowing Jerry his lone passage. Jerry feels uncertain as to whether even aggression is not a form of love. Having learnt from this incident that a simultaneous combination of love-hate is the only teaching emotion, Jerry seeks out Peter, on his way back from the zoo, in a last desperate attempt at human communication.

Jerry suddenly approaches Peter seated on his Park bench and tries to engage him in conversation. Peter, reluctant but polite, gradually gets drawn in as Jerry carefully manipulates him with his love-hate technique. Starting with personal questions, including some uncomfortable ones, Jerry goes on to narrate his own past experiences, again somewhat embarrassingly for Peter. Jerry then tries physical contact by tickling Peter disarmingly, and later manages to provoke him with insults and blows into an open fight. The final upshot of all this is that Jerry deliberately thrusts himself on the knife Peter is made to hold out in self-defence. Peter is thus violently shocked out of his habitual bourgeois complacency.

Jerry's suicide must be perceived not as a negative escape from life, but as a positive existentialist choice which succeeds in conveying to Peter the superior consciousness of the absurd. Just as Peter will never be able to forget the absurd fact that he has involuntarily killed a man, so he must henceforth acknowledge the existence of 'unaccomodated man' and grow to recognize the faces of isolation and despair. From Peter's

point of view it is a terrifying existentialist experience: the
sudden revelation of his absurd situation as a civilized human
being and a genuine insight into the totally contingent nature
of life. Jerry dies happy and satisfied in having finally established human contact, in having 'dispossessed' Peter of his
bench (i.e. his bourgeois values), and in 'converting' Peter to
an existentialist awareness. The tragic fact here is that one
human consciousness impinges on another only at the cost of
a life. Like the 'Ancient Mariner' who stopped the wedding
guest, Jerry has made out of Peter 'a sadder and a wiser man'
who must now assume the burden of the absurd.

It is as late as the mid-sixties that Arthur Miller evinces
concern for the metaphysical implications of social and contemporary issues. In *After the Fall* (1964), Miller's confessional autobiographical play encompassing the entire war
generation, Miller is still groping in the dark in his efforts to
penetrate the nature of man and the human condition. Quentin,
the protagonist, Miller's alter-ego, realizes that 'success' and
'innocence' are both forms of self-deception masking man's
egotism. On the point of his third marriage Quentin feels the
excruciating need to explore the reality of the human situation. He recalls various incidents of the betrayal of love: his
mother's selfishness and contempt for his father, Elsie's
treatment of her husband, his own self-regarding actions. In
his recognition that he mus assume total responsibility for
the choices that have shaped his life, since all mitigating
absolutes are absent, Quentin comes close to holding an
existentialist position. He is also made to discover the complex truth that inconstancy and treachery in personal relationships can somehow become mixed up with cruelty and violence
in public life, here symbolized by the tower of a German
concentration camp and the Committee on un-American
Activities. Dehumanized institutions derive their power not
only from the supposed 'innocents' who wish to remain
uninvolved, but also from the victims themselves who yield
unprotestingly.

Holga teaches Quentin the necessity of accepting complicity in guilt: "no one they didn't kill can be innocent again."
Her parable-like dream of the disgusting idiot child she
at last manages to embrace represents her own acceptance

of unpleasant truths about herself. Miller emphasizes the need to come to terms with treachery, cruelty, betrayal and guilt as basic components of human nature, to be met with pervasively in a fallen world: "What burning cities taught her and the death of love taught me: that we are very dangerous." This is comparable to Camus' perception in *The Fall* that guilt forms the human link, and accordingly, even Christ had felt the burden of guilt as the survivor of the massacre of innocents.

Miller's solution for the human predicament is a limited love that can no longer demand perfect faith, but can still bridge the separateness of human beings, if only temporarily. Quentin's movement towards Holga, at the end of the play, denotes a renewal of effort at human relationships founded on existentialist 'truth', the possibility of which Miller refuses to rule out.

Despite growing existentalist perceptions, Miller's *After the Fall* remains a rather tortuous and diffuse play, partly on account of its disjointed memory-sequence structure. Importance is given less to the 'momentous enlightenment' achieved than to the process of introspection and self-interrogation. Hence Miller's resolution seems somewhat more optimistic than the play's actual experience would allow for.

If Miller is feeling his way towards an existentialist consciousness in *After the Fall*, he may be said to have arrived at it in his next play, *Incident at Vichy* (1964), which answers to the description of Sartre's 'drama of situation'.[7] The characters, who represent different human types, are mainly Jews picked up by the Germans at random and made to wait in a bare station-like room under security guards. Tension and anxiety mount as the suspicions of the artist Lebeau are confirmed surreptitiously by the waiter that document-checking is only a cover for transporting Jews to death-camps in Poland. From the existentialist point of view, particularly as Heidegger and Sartre conceived it, man exercises his greatest freedom of choice when confronted with death. The play reveals this zero-degree consciousness of the various Nazi victims in a limit situation. LeDuc, the psychiatrist, accepts the possibility of senseless cruelty and extermination of people, not because the Germans are Fascists, but "because they are people", and violence is a fundamental component of human nature. He also makes the incisive existentialist observation that man requires a victim, simply to assert his own being: "Each man has his Jew: it is the other. And Jews have their Jews." This is factually illustrated in the play by the contemptuous treatment meted out to the Gipsy who happens to be the social outcast in the group of Jewish detenus.

The conflict between LeDuc and Von Berg once more focuses the problem of 'innocence' versus 'complicity in guilt'. Von Berg, a sensitive and refined Austrian aristocrat, has been deeply shocked by Nazi vulgarity in his own country; his past experiences have brought him to the acute existentialist realization that the Germans commit atrocities "because they are nothing . . . the less you exist the more important it is to make a clear impression." Seeing that Von Berg is likely to be released, LeDuc openly charges him with the complicity of the guilty survivor who cannot possibly share the totally meaningless suffering of the actual victims. LeDuc claims he is angry that he should "have been born before the day when man has accepted his own nature; that he is not reasonable, that he is full of murder, that his ideals are only the little tax he pays for the right to hate and kill with a clear conscience." His apparently existentialist view of human nature seems partly genuine and partly in 'bad faith' as he flings it as a challenge to Von Berg's idealistic conscience. Under the pressure of circumstances in this crisis situation Von Berg is able to take an authentic existentialist decision by surrendering his white pass to LeDuc and urging him to escape in his stead. LeDuc who is immediately overcome by his own complicity in guilt none the less decides to survive. Von Berg is seen to graduate from suicide contemplated as an escape to self-sacrifice for another individual as a correct existentialist choice, offering proof of one's own humanity and demonstrating the human link of genuine fellow feeling. His action marks a defeat for the Major who stands for cynical collaboration with the Nazis, rationalizing that he no longer cares for human love or respect "because there are no persons anymore".

So far, I have deliberately selected for discussion and analysis plays which reveal substantial existentialist content, though the overall impression remains that existentialism has not struck deep roots in the American theatre. After the debacle of the Broadway production of his play, *No Exit*, Sartre reportedly grumbled, "Americans will never understand anything about existentialism."[8] Even when appearing to be 'existentialist' the tendency of modern American drama is more towards social or psychological comment and explication than towards the exploration of man's metaphysical alienation. Since American drama is less concerned with absurdist vision than with *avant-garde* techniques and style, it is the 'theatre of the absurd' rather than existentialist drama *per se* which has proved relatively more attractive. Albee's *The American Dream* (1961), for example, provides a typical instance of the American theatre's timid liaison with existentialism.[9] On the face of it an American version of Ionesco's absurd drama, *The Bald Prima Donna* (1951), Albee's play restricts itself to travestying the stereotyped American-way-of-life without reaching out to the wider and more disturbing implications of Ionesco's theatre. Though absurdist dramatic techniques—such as non-rational events, devalued language, social euphemism, continual self-deception, imaginative cruelty and threat—are skilfully employed, they are not made to cohere and lead up to an effective undermining of all rational structures of human intercourse. Albee's aim is to locate the absurd in the accepted norms of social behaviour and in certain myths projected by the mass media, particularly American family life. As Albee himself confirms in his preface: "the play is an examination of the American Scene, an attack on the substitution of artificial for real values in our society, a condemnation of complacency, cruelty, emasculation and vacuity; it is a stand against the fiction that everything in this slipping land of ours is peachy-keen." Albee seems fully aware of the play's limited scope and makes no metaphysical claims for it. Such a social critique ultimately implies the possibility of change and betterment of society. What is remediable is not total, and this is precisely the point of divergence between existentialism and social criticism. While sociological reasons might be able to account for this situation in the theatre, modern American drama, barring a few exceptions, remains on the fringe of existentialist literature.

NOTES

1. Jean-Paul Sartre, 'Existentialism is a Humanism,' *Existentialism from Dostoevsky to Sartre*, ed. Walter Kaufmann (Cleveland : The World Publishing Company, 1956), p. 289.
2. William V. Spanos, *A Casebook on Existentialism* (New York: Thomas Y. Cromwell Company, 1966), p. 341.
3. Quoted by Robert Brustein, *The Theatre of Revolt* (Boston: Little Brown and Company, 1964), p. 339.
4. Martin Heidegger, *Being and Time*, trans. J. Macquarrie and E.S. Robinson (New York: Harper and Rowe, 1962), p. 307.
5. Quoted by Frederic I. Carpenter, *Eugene O'Neill* (Boston: Twayne Publishers, G.K. Hall & Company, rev. ed. 1979), p. 149.
6. Letter to Lawrence Langer dated August 11, 1940.
7. Jean-Paul Sartre, 'For a Theater of Situations;' 'Forgers of Myths,' reprinted *Sartre on Theater*, eds. Michel Contat and Michel Rybalka (New York: Pantheon Books, 1976), pp. 3-5; 33-43.
8. Quoted by Eric Bentley, 'Sartre's Struggle for Existenz,' *Kenyon Review*, X (1948), pp. 328-334.
9. Also listed by Spanos, *A Casebook on Existentialism*, p. 341.

6

TWO TYPES OF EXISTENTIAL EXPERIENCE IN *MOBY-DICK*

Lalita Subbu

MOBY-DICK (1851) is a novel about struggle. For Melville, the idea of struggle is complex. It is the story of American sailors on a whaling expedition—the account of man's actions. It also concerns the development of man's thought as he attempts to understand the universe. Action as well as perception are involved in the struggle. As the stories of Ahab, Ishmael and Moby-Dick unfold themselves, the conflict takes on the stature of antiquity, as it represents the ontological journey of the human soul through the ages. Ahab's tussle with Moby-Dick is the tussle of man with his existence and its mysteries. In this contest man has to live with his doubts and exercise a choice constantly. He has to choose a way of action and a way of belief.

In the stories of Ahab and Ishmael the novel shows the troubled assertion of freedom and of self by both of them. The concreteness of their subjective experience is used to shed light on the problem of existence itself. This assertion of their freedom together with the subjective quality of their existence are in themselves two aspects of the existential predicament. The fundamental loneliness of the existential hero is evident in both Ahab's and Ishmael's search for truth. Each of them has exercised his choice irrevocably: one, to fight Moby-Dick, the other, to contemplate him as a symbol of mystery. *Moby-Dick* is thus a novel where the existential experience of man is explored constantly. In exploring it, Melville has revealed his dilemmas about the universe through a series of questions.

The process of questioning yields some rich insights, but the questions themselves have no ultimate answers.

The questions Melville asks deal directly with the problem of man in the universe. What is the principle behind our existence? How does the universe regard man? How does man regard the universe? How does man regard himself? In examining these questions, the mind of the American voyager is actually engaged in a crucial act of knowledge. This knowledge acts as the fulcrum of what the voyager calls his existence. The meaning behind any object is now the centre of inquiry, as, for example, the meaning of the whale. Man is surrounded by meanings of all kinds (such as the implication of the whale, or the doubloon, or the sea). He has to explore the relationship between the implication of any idea as it hits him, and the manner in which it works upon his mind. He is now concerned with the meaning of meaning. And the meaning of meaning is a new question, not a new answer.

For there is not one meaning, but many meanings in *Moby-Dick*. Ahab's quest is a case in point. Though the novel is written at the end of the American Puritan tradition, the figure of Ahab is Biblical as well as existential. His quest itself defies categorization. On the one hand, he is damned because he is a man of "bad faith" or "despair" in the Kierkegaardian sense; on the other hand, he is committed to his search and has exercised a choice.

Kierkegaard outlines the predicament of the man of faith in the figure of Abraham in *Fear and Trembling* (1843).[1] Kierkegaard invests Abraham with grandeur on account of the "dread" Abraham feels and overcomes in sacrificing his son Isaac, for it is in acting *against* his own impulses, *against* the normal ethical code, that Abraham's heroism lies. The particular is exalted above the universal. Kierkegaard says of Abraham that his trial is the most important fact for Abraham, and it is in Abraham's link with the absolute (i.e. God) as an individual on trial that Abraham's violation of the normal code of parental love may be sanctioned. This idea is voiced by Father Mapple in *Moby-Dick*. when he says in his sermon that, "if we obey God, we must disobey ourselves, and it is in this disobeying ourselves, wherein the hardness of obeying God consists."[2] The paradox of faith is this, that the individual is

higher than the universal, that the individual determines his
relation to the universal by his relation to the absolute; not
his relation to the absolute by his relation to the universal.
For the existential hero the conventional ethical judgement of
the world becomes irrelevant.

But it is not faith that we deal with, in the case of Ahab.
It is despair, sin and isolation. Ahab talks of the capacity
that life has to unsettle even our deepest faith, when he
remarks to the body of a dead whale, "O head! thou hast seen
enough to split the planets and make an *infidel of Abraham*,
and not one syllable is thine!" (p. 418). The man of despair
suffers more than the others and feels that he has been singled
out for his suffering. Then the man of despair can turn religious or demoniac. He can submit himself to God or defy
God. A certain amount of defiance is inherent in the demoniac
man, because he sticks to his torment, rages against everything
and shies away from the will-to-be, unlike Abraham, who
undergoes the process of *becoming* by virtue of his faith.
Ahab's situation in *Moby-Dick* is peculiarly appropriate to the
idea voiced by Kierkegaard in *The Sickness Unto Death* (1849).[3]
Under the impact of despair, the existence of the demoniac
man becomes a diseased one. His condition is not just one of
physical pain, but is for the most part, characterized by mental
and metaphysical agony. Ahab is ill, but not merely through
having lost his leg. He is *spiritually* ill.

In the world of Ahab, there is no hope. This hopelessness
creates despair and anguish. The anguish results in a situation
where, though the terms "good" and "evil" retain their traditional definitions, the dividing line between them seems to
disappear, as the voyage becomes more and more "absurd" in
the existentialist sense of the word. The crew of the ship is
caught in the monomania of the captain. And the monomania
itself is the battle between a madman and a dumb animal. The
actions of Ahab seem meaningless to his crew. The world,
except for Moby-Dick and himself, seems meaningless to Ahab.

Melville constantly poses contradictions in his interpretation
of Ahab's chase and of Ahab himself. He introduces the
stories of both Job and Jonah, the one a man of faith who
is made to doubt God and the other a man of doubt who is
made to suffer for his disobedience. Jonah's story is *allegori-*

cal, but Melville's novel is *symbolic*. It is as though Melville himself will not resolve the contradictions he presents to us. The whale must remain Job's whale *as well as* Jonah's whale. It must be a symbol of divine mystery as well as of divine retribution. Ahab may be damned from an ethical point of view, though his quest may have its own validity from another point of view. Man shows temerity in questioning the universe; yet, this questioning is also inevitable, Melville seems to say. Ahab and Ishmael seek reality. Melville, in *his* turn, tries to understand the nature of the malignity that menaces life. As reality can be approached through symbols, Melville *creates* the whale, and Ahab seeks, not the actual whale alone, but the *symbolic* whale as well.

At this point, we may well ask whether Meliville's existentialism is theistic or atheistic. Is it wrong for Ahab to swear and act as he does in this "illness", or is his enquiry a profound enquiry? This is the disturbing ambivalence of Melville's treatment of the existential experience of Ahab in *Moby-Dick*. An ethical dimension is inherent in the story, with the survival of Ishmael and the death of Ahab, who demands, "Who's over me?" Ahab, in his identification with God, "Is Ahab, Ahab? Is it I, God, or who, that lifts this arm?" (p. 653) is a doomed over-reacher, and as such, suffers his fate. But his fate, nonetheless, is a search for the meaning *behind* appearances. There is a tragic cast to the existentialism of Melville in *Moby-Dick*. Ahab is no exalted Abraham, but more akin to Job and Jonah in his doubt and speculation. Melville chooses the figure of Jonah, just as Kierkegaard chooses the figure of Abraham, but with a difference. Jonah's lesson is to preach the truth to the face of falsehood. Ishmael enacts this process completely, but the awful isolation of Jonah is reserved for Ahab. The whole universe centres on Ahab's plight as on Jonah's. The whole ship is in danger because of one man.

All mortal greatness is disease, as Ishmael remarks. Ahab is "grand", "ungodly", but also "god-like". Ahab can be called existentialist in only one sense—in the passionate sincerity of his enquiry. His speculation reaches a height because he dominates the ship and transforms a natural voyage into a supernatural one. Every man must find a different meaning for himself in the whale. Every man must struggle to seek the solution to his narcissistic reflection in the water. In grasping the "ungraspable phantom of life" man is both a solipsist and a seer. The dangers of solipsism are described in the Narcissus myth which shows a baffled self-scrutiny, but at the same time, we must recognize that few men have the courage of Ahab to penetrate through the "visible" layers to the "invisible" ones beneath. Ahab reflects, to some extent, his creator's vacillation between the two poles of belief and doubt.

The question aries whether Ahab or Ishmael is right, or whether both are right. Despair is negative, as in the case of Ahab, but if the despair has to end, the truth behind the object of Ahab's inquiry must be known. To know the truth *behind* the object, he must pierce *through* the object itself. Ahab's action becomes a point of debate. His act is 'absurd' as it is not understood by the world. In Kierkegaard's account of Abraham, Abraham's action is in danger of being misunderstood by ordinary ethical standards. But we know that Abraham's action is right, and that for him, the significance of his own predicament is greater than the general ethical stand. He is a cruel father to the world, but a true servant of God to himself. Similarly, Ahab is condemned by Ishmael and Starbuck as he seems to violate morality itself in his fanatical pursuit of the whale. But his experience is valid in an existentialist sense, though it does not conform to ethical norms. His heroism takes its starting point from a rejection of traditional piety and traditional knowledge.

A careful scrutiny of Ahab's arguments shows that his despair is grounded in external as well as internal causes. The man of despair, according to Kierkegaard, knows up to a point that he is in despair. He notices it in himself as one notices in oneself that one is going about with an illness as yet unpronounced, but he will not quite admit what illness it is. Yet Ahab admits that for this hunt his "malady" is his most "desired health". He is "queer . . . very queer", as his crew pronounces, but his insanity is, paradoxically, a form of sanity to him : "All loveliness is anguish to me, since I can ne'er enjoy . . . damned, most subtly and malignantly ! damned in the midst of Paradise ! What I've dared, I've willed; and what I've willed, I'll do ! They think me mad . . . but I'm demoniac, I am madness maddened! That wild madness that's only calm to comprehend itself" (p. 266).

What the novel shows us is the manner in which Ahab endows the event of the loss of his leg with a deep significance. He thinks he is in despair about something earthly and constantly talks about it, and yet he is *actually* in despair about the *eternal*. Like Sartre's heroes, Ahab faces two problems. On the one hand, he cannot be separated from his obsession, which is Moby-Dick; the obsession *is* Ahab. On the other hand, he feels the strangest isolation, because his *internal* reality constitutes all that he *is*; his external reality constitutes all that he is *not*. In Ishmael's analysis of Ahab's monomania, we can see this :

> Ahab had cherished a wild vindictiveness against the whale, all the more fell for that in his frantic morbidness he at last came to identify with him, not only all his bodily woes, but all his intellectual and spiritual exasperations. The White Whale swam before him as the monomaniac incarnation of all those malicious agencies. . . . All that most maddens and torments . . . all truth with malice in it . . . all the subtle demonisms of life and thought; all evil, to crazy Ahab, were visibly personified, and made practically assailable in Moby-Dick (p. 283).

Ahab's obsession with the whale unites him with Moby-Dick, but separates him from his countrymen. His consciousness sees disjunction and disrelation between himself and the world.

The force behind Ahab's speculations about the universe is contained in his enquiry into its arbitrary nature. What kind of justice was operative in the universe that used the whale to dismember him ? The perception behind man's detection of arbitrariness in the universe is an existentialist one, as is revealed by Kierkegaard in his experimental novel, *Repetition*, where he questions this point :

> Who am I ? . . . How did I come into the world ? Why was I not consulted, why not made acquainted with its manners and customs . . . ? And if I am to be compelled to take part in it, where is the director ? I should like to make a remark to him . . . [4]

In the face of such a universe, Ahab feels the need to strike hard through the pasteboard mask.

It must be pointed out here that Ahab attributes malice to the whale. The whale himself is not inherently malicious. To some extent, Ahab's is a philosophical enquiry. For him, truth has *no* confines. He feels the whale to be that inhibiting wall which imprisons him : "All visible objects . . . are but as pasteboard masks. But in . . . the living act, the undoubted deed . . . some unknown but still reasoning thing puts forth the mouldings of its features from behind the unreasoning mask If man will strike, strike through the mask ! How can the prisoner reach outside except by thrusting through the wall ?" (p. 262). Even if there is nothingness behind the mask, Ahab believes in the value of the exploration itself.

The value attached to any existentialist exploration is in the pursuit of an absolute which is the object of that exploration. Jean-Paul Sartre, in a compelling essay on *Moby-Dick*, locates Melville's absolute in the whiteness of the whale. This whiteness, Sartre points out, is a *leitmotiv* of demoniacal horror, but is also the absolute which confronts Ahab and Ishmael. In being condemned to live at the level of Being, Ahab and Ishmael have to return to this whiteness—this absolute. It is interesting that the whale, which is on one level of interpretation, a manifestation of divinity, is singled out by Sartre, an atheistic existentialist, as expressing what he calls an absolute : "We haunt the absolute," Sartre says, "but no one to my knowledge, no one except Melville has attempted this extraordinary undertaking of retaining the taste of a particular quality (i. e. whiteness) and seeking in it the absolute which goes beyond it."[5] The whale is important because it defies the human intellect. It is the unsourced existence of man, and in thinking and rethinking about it man attempts to fathom its meaning. The while approximates Reality.

But Reality, through Melville's responses to it, emerges both as a vision of the solitary ego as well as one of plurality in the universe. Ahab's interpretation of the doubloon illustrates the first kind of reality : "The firm tower, that is Ahab; the volcano, that is Ahab; the courageous, the undaunted, and victorious fowl, that, too, is Ahab; all are

Ahab" (p. 541). The second kind of reality is illustrated by the vision of Pip, the mad black boy, who interprets the doubloon as the multiplicity of life : "I look, you look he looks . . ." (p. 545). Similarly, we may go on to point out that the whale is divine for Ishmael, but evil for Ahab.

Ishmael points out that in the whole of Ahab's madness, not one jot of his great natural intellect perishes. He is frighteningly sane. The only imbalance that Ahab reflects is in magnifying a partial truth (the truth of evil) into the *whole* truth. There is both good and evil in the world, as we learn from Ishmael. The Manichean belief in the two halves of the universe (the good and evil), is only partially understood by Ahab. For him, the universe is evil, as the whale "tasks" him. To Ahab, the whale is all-destroying, but not all-conquering. In his own action and the assertion behind it, Ahab defies the whale to the end and does not relinquish the chase, though he himself is dying. The action becomes both more valuable and more poignantly self-defeating, as it is Ahab's isolation that has paid the price for it :

> Oh, lonely death on lonely life ! Oh, now I feel my topmost greatness lies in my topmost grief !" (p. 684)

Ahab's interpretation of Moby-Dick as being an evil principle has a peculiar status in the novel. The novel cannot validate his theory but it does not invalidate it either. Melville shows both the grandeur of the self-assertion behind Ahab's exploration *and* the precarious isolation of his fixed interpretation of the whale, especially when confronted with the plurality of meanings in the universe. Ishmael, as narrator, sustains the two-fold response to Ahab.

Ishmael can analyse Ahab because Ishmael, too, has an existentialist role to play. Both he and Ahab recognize that the universe is capricious. For Ishmael, this caprice is not a matter for worry : "There are certain queer times and occasions in this strange mixed affair we call life when a man takes this whole universe for a vast practical joke, though the wit thereof he but dimly discerns, and more than suspects that the joke is at nobody's expense but his own" (p. 329). Ahab's reaction is more akin to the reaction voiced by man in Stephen Crane's poem :

> A man said to the universe: 'Sir, I exist !'
> 'However,' replied the universe,
> The fact has not created in me
> A sense of obligation.'[6]

There are some differences in the attitudes of Ishmael and Ahab towards the universe. Ishmael is not tormented by the indifference of the universe as Ahab is. He sees the whale primarily as Job's whale, a mystery that is not to be unravelled. The cosmic quality of the whale is perceived by Ishmael and hence he will not chase it. Ahab's attitude is different. He says he will strike even the sun if it insults him. One may notice the difference between Ahab and a later American hero, Santiago, the hero of Hemingway's *The Old Man and the Sea*. Both *Moby-Dick* and Hemingway's novel deal with the chase of a creature at sea. However, though Santiago is as determined to catch his fish as Ahab is determined to catch Moby-Dick, he expresses not existential defiance but an acceptance of the impossibility of achieving eternal goals :

> The fish is my friend . . . But I must kill him . . . I do not understand these things, he thought. But it is good that we do not have to try and kill the sun, or the moon or the stars. It is quite enough to live on the sea and kill our true brothers.[7]

In defying the whale, Ahab achieves self-expression, but in battling against what he believes to be evil with power instead of love, he becomes the image of the thing he hates, and so perishes. In hunting the whale, Ahab is hunting *himself*, because to some extent *he is* the hunt and the *purpose* of the hunt, as Narcissus was to himself. Ahab can apprehend reality only vis-a-vis his own torment which he feels, and Ishmael can speculate upon it only in terms of his own "dread"— his feeling that life is made up of ambivalent impulses. Moby-Dick may be evil, but is also good. The ocean may be sharkish, but it is also safe.

In Ishmael's constant attempt to mediate between the "calm" core of his own Being and the "storms" and "tornadoes" also present, Melville tries to show how man tries to move from one mode of existence to another. So, if we look for a final solution to the problems of how the universe regards man and how man regards the universe, the novel unsettles us constantly. If Melville is theoretically indecisive about the meaning of the experience he conveys in *Moby-Dick*, it is because the experience is fundamentally untranslatable. In its enormity, the novel encompasses opposing tendencies. On the one hand, Ahab wages war, and the war brings pain to him. He dies defeated. But, on the other hand, *though* he dies defeated, he still retains the dignity of an explorer who searches for the truth of the universe around him and the truth of his own experiences.

Ahab moves within a framework that is partly ethical and partly symbolic. The moral scheme of the novel damns him and saves Ishmael. But the meaning, or the meanings, of life that unsettle the moral code, also argue for the validity of his search for the truth about existence. Ahab's commitment is to some extent existentialist, as it is born of the desire to express the independence of his self in a world that to him has lost meaning. Though his quest is not the only quest in the novel, it has the truth of subjective experience. The decisive point is that Ahab is committed to his quest with passionate sincerity. He may be related to a quest that is false according to moral or ethical standards, but if his passion for the quest is *not* false, we may regard him as an existentialist hero.

NOTES

1. Soren Kierkegaard, *Fear and Trembling* (1843), in *Fear and Trembling and The Sickness Unto Death*, trans. and introd. Walter Lowrie (Princeton: Princeton University Press, 1954).
2. Herman Melville, *Moby-Dick: Or, The Whale*, ed. and introd. Harold Beaver (1851; rpt. Harmondsworth: Penguin Books, 1972), p. 136. Further references to this text are given within parentheses.
3. Kierkegaard, *The Sickness Unto Death* (1849), in *Fear and Trembling and The Sickness Unto Death*, trans. and introd. Walter Lowrie (Princeton: Princeton University Press, 1954).
4. Soren Kierkegaard, *Repetition* (Princeton, 1946). The passage is quoted by Paul Brodtkorb, Jr., in Notes to his book, *Ishmael's White World: A Phenomenological Reading of "Moby-Dick"* (New Haven and London: Yale University Press, 1965), p. 162.

5. Jean-Paul Sartre, "Herman Melville's *Moby-Dick*," (1941), in *Twentieth Century Interpretations of "Moby-Dick*," ed. Michael T. Gilmore (Englewood Cliffs, New Jersey: Prentice-Hall, Inc., 1977), p. 95.
6. Stephen Crane's poem is quoted by Nelson J. Smith in his *Pennant Key-Indexed Study Guide to Melville's "Moby-Dick"* (Philadelphia and New York: Educational Research Associates Inc., in association with Bantam Books, Inc., 1967), p. 84.
7. Ernest Hemingway, *The Old Man and the Sea* (1952; rpt. Harmondsworth: Penguin Books, 1966), p. 66.

7

HYACINTH ROBINSON'S EXISTENTIAL CHOICE

Malashri Lal

HENRY JAMES'S *The Princess Casamassima*, published in 1886, is a story supposedly reflecting anarchist politics in England in the 1880s. James's "politics" is however too diffuse to entrench the novel in the social milieu. Characteristically, James confessed to his greater interest in using a *disponible*, an individual medium of consciousness, to explore the implications of radicalism. When writing the Preface to the novel, the author was pleased to observe that he had adhered to a wise principle of narrative technique: ". . . clearness and concreteness constantly depend, for any pictorial whole, on same *concentrated* individual notation of them".[1] Scenes, chacraters, situations crowded the imagination during James's "perambulations" through the city, and then one day, says James, "little Hyacinth Robinson—he sprang up for me out of the London pavement."[2] The other principal character, Princess Casamassima, emerged from James's desire to "resuscitate" Christina Light, the enigmatic and destructive heroine of *Roderick Hudson* who had "known herself striking, in an earlier connexion, and couldn't resign herself not to strike again."[3]

Hyacinth Robinson is a recognizable Jamesian figure— imaginative, idealistic, gifted with a fine consciousness—who meets his tragedy in being manipulated by those whom he trusts. Yet, he is unique in the James canon as the only "hero" who ends his life by self-inflicted violence when his cherished belief in the sanctity of personal relationships is shattered. Moreover, the suicide of Hyacinth is the second death with which the Princess is associated. Though James retained an ambiguity about the manner of Roderick Hudson's death in an Alpine storm, and one is never sure whether Roderick went over the precipice by accident or deliberation, there is no uncertainty about Hyacinth Robinson's act of self-destruction.

This paper examines Hyacinth Robinson's suicide as the inevitable culmination of an existential dilemma in which James places "the little London book-binder." One may recall Albert Camus' figure of the existential man: "I don't know whether this world has a meaning that transcends it . . . . I can understand only in human terms. What I touch, what resists me—that is what I understand. And these two certainties—my appetite for the absolute and for unity and the impossibility of reducing this world to a rational and reasonable principle—I also know I cannot reconcile them."[4] Hyacinth Robinson, James's "limited vessel of consciousness," tries to understand the world in "human terms," and the Princess Casamassima assumes the role of his mentor. When his noble vision of a perfect social order stands revealed as an impossibility, Hyacinth still struggles to understand the dialectics of socialism and elitism. Furthermore, in the story of Hyacinth Robinson, James links up the notion of suicide as a political gesture and suicide resulting from personal imperatives. James said in the Preface to *The Princess Casamassima,* "Experience, as I see it, is our apprehension and our measure of what happens to us as social creatures," and related this observation to Hyacinth's tragedy that "something more personal than his opinion and his vows, becomes the sharpest of his torments."[5] Thus the novel dramatizes the process by which Hyacinth's illusions about a rational world order are destroyed, and brings it to the climactic moment when Hyacinth stands poised at the brink of a spiritual void.

In offering this interpretation of the novel, it is obvious that I am relegating the "politics" of *The Princess Casamassima* to a secondary place and giving importance to what T.S. Eliot called "the deeper psychology" of a Jamesian novel.

This paper explores Hyacinth Robinson's private conflict with the publicly avowed position of the anarchists with whom he is supposedly in league. Against this background, Hyacinth's existential dilemma arises.

Trilling's formulation of "a literary tradition of the Young Man from the Provinces," is brilliant and persuasive. Hyacinth Robinson belongs to a generic "type" which is characterized thus:

> He need not come from the provinces in literal fact, his social class may constitute his province. But a provincial birth and rearing suggest the simplicity and the high hopes he begins with—he starts with a great demand upon life and a great wonder about its complexity and promise.[6]

Trilling goes on to say, "The province from which Hyacinth Robinson comes is a city slum"; and thus one meets James's only proletarian hero, the common man gifted with intelligence and limited by circumstances, compelled to eke out an existence by practising a trade. In terms of Sartre's statement that "man first of all exists, encounters himself, surges up in the world—and defines himself afterwards,"[7] Hyacinth's early years at Miss Pynsent's house in Lomax Place are his phase of simple existence when he is unaware of the potential within himself. He has the makings of an existential figure. Mr. Vetch, the fiddler, describes him as, "a thin-skinned, morbid, mooning, introspective little beggar, with a good deal of imagination and not much perserverence, who'll expect a good deal more of life than he'll find in it" (p. 44).[8]

The early stirrings of political interest come from Hyacinth's boredom with the monotony of humdrum domesticity. But, when Hyacinth's radical friends ask an apparently simple question about his social origins, the novel begins to delve into the fundamental meaning of identity:

> 'Perhaps you're French' suggested the strange young man. . .
> . . . He found it a difficult pass, partly because there was something exciting and embarassing in the attention of the other visitor, and partly because he had never yet had to decide that important question. . . . Our young friend was under a cloud and a stigma, but he was not yet prepared to admit he was ridiculous. 'Oh, I dare say I ain't anything,' he replied in a moment (p. 96).

The issue can no longer be evaded after Hyacinth meets the Princess Casamassima and is captivated by her beauty, intelligence and wealth. The socialist cause itself seems to glow with the promise of a perfect future when the charming Princess mingles with the rugged group of anarchists. Hyacinth's association with the Princess and his suspicion that their mutual attraction is inspired by a shared political belief, but is also personal, brings Hyacinth to the most important stage of his consciousness. In existential language, Hyacinth "encounters himself—surges up in the world."

Even as one applies the terminology of Existentialism to James's novel, it would be well to remember Camus's warning, "For everything begins with consciousness and nothing is worth anything except through it. There is nothing original about these remarks." "Consciousness" is James's primary interest, but in *The Princess Casamassima*, James, unlike modern existentialists, sets up the encounter with the self in terms of its encounter with another figure.

The Princess is a *femme fatale*, as James inplies in his Preface, whose superficial brilliance lures her victims to disaster. It is Hyacinth's dangerous tendency that he romanticizes the Princess. She is the feminine mystique composed "of every element of loveliness, every delicacy of feature, every shade and tone that contributed to charm" (p. 267). James's decriptions of her exterior beauty are counterbalanced by hints of her deep-rooted urge for power. The Princess is a figure of "everlasting" beauty (p. 267), she is also untroubled by "decent human feeling, what's commonly called a bit of heart" (p. 305). In many subtle ways, she uses her beauty and wealth to attract and destroy the men who interest her.

The heroine's admirers are arranged as a sequence of increasing challenge. The artist figure, Roderick Hudson, had been easily captivated by the beauty of physical form; to the Prince whom Christina marries, she had seemed like the time-honoured majestic consort to royalty. Christina's socialist tendencies date from that time. As a "Princess" she feels "caught" in a form of *mariage de convenance* and reacts to the boredom of the aristocratic life. Some diversion is offered by Captain Sholto who is happy to escort the "cleverest woman in Europe" though knowing that "she will act out

her extra-ordinary nature" (p. 305) to his disadvantage. Hyacinth Robinson and Paul Muniment bring to Christina's life the
first opportunity to break away from her restricted class associations and she entertains this as a fresh challenge to her
feminine wiles.

The Princess Casamassima is primarily a study of the
relation between a poor and artistically gifted man and a rich,
beautiful woman. It depicts their search for a common ground
for contact whereby the discriminations of birth may be obliterated. Political anarchism, with its avowed interest in root-
ing out class differences, holds attraction for the Princess and
for Hyacinth. It becomes their medium for investigating
and understanding each other's spheres of existence; it is their
mode of exploring each other's sensibilities, beliefs and values.
The anarchist movement is the crucible in which their diverse
emotions form new components and emerge with new meanings. Herein, I agree with F.O. Matthiessen's statement that
James is interested "solely in the personal problem, in what
happens when his sensitive lower-class hero is distracted from
his revolutionary convictions by his desire to establish a social
—not less than socialist connexion."[9]

Evil issues from the manipulative power of wealth. Paradoxically, money gives status, yet a declared regard for it is
an uncouth sentiment. The political rebels clamour for the
equitable distribution of wealth but need financing to translate
their theories into propaganda and practice. The Princess
Casamassima recognizes the power of wealth and acts accordingly.

The revolutionaries are attracted by her money, even
Hoffendahl, the elusive leader of the political underworld, is
known personally to her. She however finds an inconspicuous
subject for experimenting with her assets of wealth and beauty.
This is Hyacinth Robinson, a bookbinder from an obscure
London slum, whose artistic taste is as obvious as his poverty.
She finds him attractive for several reasons. First, she is
curious to see if an artistic consciousness can be heightened
by the study of art heritage. Sh therefore leads Hyacinth to
a vista of treasured antiquary and enacts the role of an
aristocratic patron of the arts. Secondly, on the moral side,
Christina finds an opportunity to redeem her past by offering

the spoils of her *mariage de convenance* to a poor man of receptive consciousness. Thirdly, transcending her immediate interest in Hyacinth, she is curious about the working class because of her avowed commitment to socialism. She romanticizes the preoccupations of the poor because their way of life has been a closed door beyond which lie well-guarded secrets. Hyacinth holds the key to those mysteries and, associating with him, Christina enters the world of Millicent Henning, Paul Muniment and Eustache Poupin. As directly as possible, she hears the rumblings of political discontent.

But James passes well beyond rationally identifiable factors. Strange parallels are recorded in the heredity of the Princess and her bookbinder suggesting that their attraction for each other and to the socialist cause may have originated in the situations of their birth.

Hyacinth is psychologically conditioned by his mingled blood from a "long descended supercivilized sire" and a "passionate plebian mother" (p. 429). Reaching the darkest corners of his memory he sees himself as a young boy recoiling from the dark, oppressive atmosphere of a prison house where a gross, dying woman demanded his affection. Later, his adoptive mother Pinnie, belonging to the respectable working-class stock, had erased those unpleasant memories of destitution and had raised him with care, even deference. As a curious adolescent, Hyacinth had pieced together the facts of his origin and very soon reconciled to the conflicts raging within him:

> There were times when he said to himself that it might very well be his fate to be divided to the point of torture, to be split open by sympathies that pulled him in different ways, for hadn't he an extra-ordinarily mingled current in his blood, and from the time he could remember wasn't there half of him always either playing tricks on the other or getting snubs and pinches from it? (p. 134)

The Princess is herself the product of a mixed marriage. As the daughter of an American adventurer and an Italian count, her memories of childhood also recall instability and insecurity:

> She had led from her youngest years a wandering Bohe-
> mian life in a thousand different places . . . and largely at
> one period in Rome (p. 213).

She had not known the exhilaration of freedom, only the
constraints of submitting to the worst form of European compulsion, "being married by her people, in a mercenary way, for
the sake of fortune and a great name" (p. 213).

Thus, James devises the grounds of reciprocity for Hyacinth
and the Princess Casamassima in conditions which defy rational control. The novel's dialectics elaborate these genetic
determinants in the principal figures.

Lord Frederick and Florentine represent, schematically,
Hyacinth's attraction and repulsion towards anarchism. He
sympathizes with the sordid life of the poor, yet suspects that
behind the ideals of political revolution lies an "ulcer of envy"
(p. 361). As a counterpart, Christina is lured by the rhetoric of
rebellion but is unable to forego the luxuries of the rich. As
a sort of a revenge upon the sterile, decadent aristocracy with
whom she has associated by marriage, she offers some benefits
of the family fortune to the rebels.

The paradox of fate determines that the Princess has money
and romanticizes the life of the working people, Hyacinth is
poor and glorifies the life of the rich. In some ways they try
to exchange their situations and find temporary happiness in
their escape from inherited conditions. Hyacinth enjoys an
ecstasy of oblivion when he visits the Princess at Medley.

> He rambled an hour in breathless ecstasy . . . tasting the
> fragrant air and stopping everywhere, in murmuring rap-
> ture, at the touch of some exquisite impression (p. 262).

Similarly, the Princess bursts into joyous rapture as she walks
through streets of London in her condition of assumed
poverty.

> She stopped . . . to look into the windows of vulgar est-
> ablishments and amused herself with picking out the
> abominable objects she should like to possess; selecting
> them from a new point of view, that of a reduced fortune

and the domestic arrangements of the lower middle class, and deriving extreme diversion from the idea that she now belonged to that aggrieved body (p. 373).

The crucial difference between Hyacinth and Christina is in their adherence to the principles they had professed. There is an uncomfortable note of falsity in the Princess's attempts to adopt the ways of the poor. Having realized that it is "preposterous for a woman to associate herself with the great uprising of the poor and yet live in palatial halls" (p. 270), she moves into a small house in Madeira Crescent with a low "stucco-fronted edifice" and a parlour "ornamented" with stuffed birds, an alabaster Cupid and wax flowers. James's remarks indicate that Christina is indulging in game-playing, much like the princesses of old dressing as poor shepherdesses for amusement. Madame Grandoni and Assunta, the "working class" attendants of the Princess, know that she is indulging in a passing fancy and "what on earth will it matter tomorrow." Hyacinth, innocently impressed by the Princess's ability to live with squalidness, anxiously asks Madame Grandoni, "Hasn't she sold all her beautiful things?" The practical old woman answers wryly, "She has kept a few. They're put away" (p. 376).

Towards the end of the story, the sham of the play acting is revealed for what it is. The Princess wearies of Hyacinth and is attracted to Paul Muniment. When her husband, the Prince, puts a stop to Christina's allowances, she has neither the conviction nor the courage to live genuinely like the poor, but returns submissively to the decandent aristocracy whose spirtual emptiness she knows and abhors.

The Princess, despite her fraudulent nature, benefits Hyacinth. She brings to him the world of the intellect—the literature, history and art of ancient Europe—and his sensitive imagination absorbs quickly. He is in readiness for an even fuller vision of what the human spirit can achieve when "raised to the noblest and richest expression."

Hyacinth's visit to Paris and Venice confirms his latent attraction towards the artistic heritage of the past that only aristocratic wealth would have made possible. He realizes that he must make a dreadful choice. Either he remains loyal to the anarchist cause and becomes an agent for destroying the precious heritage, or he recognizes the decadence of the modern aristocracy and wrenches from them the means of constructing a more equitable society. The thematic debate expressed through Hyacinth's visit to Europe is that the "fabric of civilization" is inextricably bound up with "despotisms" and "rapacities of the past," that monuments of learning and taste have been reared upon coercive authority (p. 352). The undeniable analogue between art and wealth is a fact of history. Walking down the Champs de Elysees and the Place de la Concorde James's book-binder recalls through the "legend of the French revolution" the opposition between the excellences of art and the ideals of democracy.

Although James portrays Hyacinth as a political idealist at the beginning of the story he shows later the clear, rational way in which he is capable of evaluating the alternatives once he understands the issues:

> The flood of democrarcy was rising over the world; that it would sweep all the traditions of the past before it; that whatever it might fail to bring, it would at least carry in its bosom a magnificent energy; and that it might be trusted to look after its own. When this high healing uplifting tide should cover the world and float into the new era, it would be its own fault (whose else?) if want and suffering and crime should continue to be ingredients of the human lot? (p. 428)

Having arrived at a statement of alternatives, Hyacinth finds himself in what I have earlier called an "existential" dilemma, for he has "encountered himself" to find "the impossibility of reducing this world to a rational and reasonable principle." Hyacinth is the only anarchist who realizes that anarchism will bring no permanent solutions, that indeed the phase of violence that he has been encouraged to participate in may set the pattern for a series of futile destructive actions in the future. Consequently, neither the destitution of the poor will be alleviated nor will the heritage of the past be preserved. In contrast to Hyacinth's search for a realistic political philosophy stands Paul Muniment's convinced radicalism, Eust-

ache Poupin's "humanitary and idealistic" notions and the
Princess Casamassima's platitude, "I'm one of those who
believe that a great new deal is destined to take place
and that it can't make things worse than they are already"
(p. 387).

It is interesting therefore to see what James makes of
Hyacinth's carefully reasoned assessment of the projected
rebellion. By the accident of birth, he remains dedicated to
both extremes of the social scale, but he cannot so divide his
loyalties and still escape some kind of violence. He is confronted by the existential choice—"there is no legislator but
himself: that he himself, thus abandoned, must decide for
himself" his personal path of "liberation."[10] He is defeated
by the enormous implications of his dilemma. Unable to
repudiate the promise to the anarchists made at the stage of
a lesser understanding of life, he turns the violent act to himself.

The manner of Hyacinth's death reflects the failure of
political idealism and also reveals the nature of his personal
tragedy. Hyacinth receives orders from Hoffendahl to assas-
sinate a member of the British aristocracy. A pistol accom-
panies the directive. Hyacinth is overwhelmed by the richness
of Europe's artistic heritage and troubled by the knowledge
of the social injustice on which the art was nurtured. Spiritually he feels committed to the aristocracy, by honour, he is
bound to the socialist cause. He shrinks from making a final
choice, prevaricates to the extent possible, then seeks out the
Princess to share his trouble and resolve his dilemma. Waiting
by the roadside for the absent Princess, Hyacinth meets another lurking, waiting figure, the Prince Casamassima. The
estranged husband, far from being a brutal, highhanded
aristocrat, turns out to be a mild, somewhat tragic man humiliated by his wife's occasional infidelities. Together the Prince
and Hyacinth watch as the Princess returns home and stands
framed in a spot of light with her latest admirer—Paul Muniment. Hyacinth flees from the dual betrayal of his love and
his political idealism to seek the council of his own conscience.
In loneliness and despair he pulls the revolutionary's trigger
at himself, blotting out the dark confusion within his turbulent
self.

James called Hyacinth Robinson a "limited vessel of consciousness." Hyacinth Robinson has not the spiritual strength to "live" through his darkest crisis. His suicide is "acceptance at its extremes" as Camus would call it, for it is a refusal to persist against the contradictions in the human condition.[11] The novel ends with an un-Jamesian finality. Hyacinth, lying in a pool of blood, and the Princess Casamassima, grieving over him, seem to make a final exchange of sentiments in their long association of reciprocities. Hyacinth, "the Young Man from the Provinces," understands the rot underlying "civilization"; the Princess, the city sophisticate, learns too late the worth of innocence and simple de votio.

NOTES

1. *The Art of the Novel : Critical Prefaces by Henry James* ed. Richard P. Blackmur (New York : Charles Scribner's Sons, 1934), p. 69.
2. *Ibid.*, p. 60.
3. *Ibid.*, p. 74.
4. *The Myth of Sisyphus* (1942), translated by Justin O'Brien (New York: Vintage Books, Random House, 1955), p. 38.
5. *The Art of the Novel*, pp. 64-65, p. 72.
6. *The Liberal Imagination* (New York: Charles Scribner's Sons, 1976), p. 611.
7. Jean-Paul Sartre, *Either/Or* (1843). Quoted from *The Modern Tradition : Backgrounds of Modern Literature*, ed. Richard Ellman and Charles Feidelson, Jr. (New York: Oxford University Press, 1945), p. 828.
8. Page numbers in parentheses refer to *The Princess Casamassima* (Middlesex: Penguin Books Ltd.), 1977. This reprints the text of the New York edition.
9. *The James Family* (New York: Alfred A. Knopf, 1947), p. 592.
10. Jean-Paul Sartre, *Existentialism and Humanism*. Quoted from *The Modern Tradition*, p. 870.
11. *The Myth of Sisyphus*, p. 40.

8

SEIZE THE DAY: AN EXISTENTIALIST LOOK

J.N. Sharma

BELLOW had read much in modern European existentialism before he wrote his first novel *Dangling Man* (1944). And Sartre's *Being and Nothingness* was first published in French in 1943. I don't know that he had read it before he wrote his first novel. That is perhaps not very important. But Bellow did write in an intellectual climate pervaded by the raw material of existentialism—a climate marked by the loss of traditional faith, the sense of a hostile, indifferent or absurd universe and the consequent need for man to turn to his own, inner resources. This ethos is clearly refleted in *Dangling Man* and Bellow's second novel *The Victim* (1947). In *Seize the Day* (1956) this view of man and his world appears in a more subtle and complex form.

There are various strands in existentialist philosophy and it will be hard to find two existentialist thinkers with identical views on all elements that their thought covers. There are often sharp convergences and, in any case, important differences in emphasis. But one view that could be perhaps called cardinal to this body of thought is that "the possibility of choice is the central fact of human nature". It is from this angle that I wish to examine *Seize the Day*. Almost all of Bellow's fiction dramatises what has come to be known as modern man's predicament—his loss of moorings and of a sense of community, his feeling of alienation from a world which he finds absurd and the despair resulting from these. But a concern with what Bellow himself has called man's "subangelic" nature is also a persistent presence in all his fiction. As Bellow himself has said in the context of modern fiction:

> The dread is great, the soul is small; man might be godlike but he is wretched; the heart should be open but it is sealed by fear. If man wretched by nature is represented, what we have here is only accurate reporting. But if it is man in the image of God, man a little lower than the angels who is impotent, the case is not the same. And it is the second assumption, the subangelic one, that writers generally make. For they are prone, as Nietzsche said in *Human, All Too Human*, to exaggerate the value of human personality. I don't know whether exaggeration is quite the word, but what it suggests we can certainly agree with. Why should wretched man need power or wish to inflate himself with imaginary glory? If this is what power signifies it can only be vanity to suffer from impotence. On the nobler assumption he should have at least sufficient power to overcome ignominy and to complete his own life. His suffering, feebleness, servitude then have a meaning. This is what writers have taken to be the justification of power. It should reveal the greatness of man. And if no other power will do this, the power of the imagination will take the task upon itself.[1]

This was said in 1957 in an essay called "Distractions of a Fiction Writer", which is a vital document to an understanding of Bellow's thinking on modern fiction in general and his own fiction in particular.

Seize the Day belongs to a later and, as Bellow himself has said, different mood than *Dangling Man* and *The Victim*. And although Bellow feels that the state of mind underlying *Seize the Day* was the same as that which produced the two earlier novels, he nevertheless sees the later novel as an advance, in terms of its affirmative quality, on the earlier two. Critics, however, generally tend to see all three as belonging to the same group, and if some identify this group as consisting of victim-protagonists, others see them as projecting beyond despair and making an optimistic comment on the human condition. The titles—*Dangling Man* and *The Victim*—are themselves explicitly suggestive of alienation, uncertainty and despair. And much of what happens to the protagonists would seem to justify this reading. But such a reading takes into account only one aspect of the protagonist's situation— his alienation and despair in *Dangling Man*, and his uncertainty and struggle for self-identity in *The Victim*. In the existentialist outlook, man's encounter with the world around and with his own self is crucial and to that extent both these novels are suffused with the existentialist atmosphere. As some critics of Bellow have recognised, the other existentialist step—exercise of the will, the making of a choice and the end of alienation—is also, though in a subdued way, present in these novels. It seems to me that the bulk of these short novels being given over to the protagonist's despair and his rather hopeless-looking struggle, the quiet, almost muffled, note signifying the choice to affirm possibility and to connect himself with humankind is overlooked. In both *Dangling Man* and *The Victim* the protagonist squarely and comprehensively encounters himself. In both a measure of success in the assertion of the will is achieved. Joseph's final recognition that without the externally imposed order of the Army he cannot cope with his life, and Asa Leventhal's anguished struggle to determine his own responsibility for Albee's misfortunes and his assertion of his self against Albee's assaults, somewhat redeem these two novels from terminating simply at stage one of the existentialist encounter with life. Curiously, most Bellow critics tend to see *Seize the Day* in the same terms. They base the reading of the novel on a squint-eyed view of Tommy Wilhelm. Abraham Kaplar, for example, feels that "none of Bellow's characters is weaker or more of a 'slob' as Tommy's father has called him."[2] And Patrick Morrow finds Tommy "almost totally to blame for his predicament. He has none of the characteristics of the successful Bellow hero, but is overwhelmed by a threat of his own making—he meets life with a constant chord of self-pity." Morrow continues: "It is evident that Tommy is comfortable in the role of perennial loser, that he *courts* defeat, finding a secure identity as a loose figure sprawling across the bosom of society, prone to seizures of self-pity. His onanism motivates

his shirking in situations of risk. He wants his father's for-
giveness in order to obtain sanction for continuing his career
in self-pity."[3]

It seems to me that Tommy Wilhelm, the protagonist of
Seize the Day, represents an advance on the two earlier novels
by more fully enacting the choice-making stage in existentialist
terms. Though he may often be a victim in his own eyes, his
conduct and actions are usually not just those of a victim, and
his being a victim, to the extent he is one, is necessary to his
breaking out of his isolation and forging a bond with what
Bellow so often calls "humankind."

The case for Tommy being a victim rests on his being a
failure in life. All his successive ventures have ended in
financial insecurity and alienation from the family, and finally
from society. When the novel opens he is forty-four, jobless
separated from his wife and children, living in a hotel inhabited
mainly by retired people, and is fast running out of his money.
By the end of the day on which the novel focusses he is totally
out of money, has the hotel bill to pay and send support
money to his wife.

An individual's life, existentialist thinkers say, is made up
of a series of choices. Let us consider the different possible
choices available to Tommy at different stages in his life and
the courage involved in making the ones he makes. His first
significant choice is made when he quits college in his
sophomore year for an acting career in Hollywood. The
initiative comes from a talent scout but he finally goes, in
defiance of the negative screen test and against his parents'
advice. Seven years of steady failure in Hollywood forces him
to try a more ordinary means of income. When he returns
home his parents are willing to send him to the medical school.
But he does not feel up to it and makes another major choice
in taking up the job of a salesman of kids' playthings. He does
reasonably well and even expects to be promoted to an executive
position. But the executive position is given to the boss's rela-
tive and he resigns his job. The act of resignation is another
major choice. Things do not go well between him and his wife,
and making another choice, he separates from her. His next
choice is made when, on Tamkin's advice, he invests $700, all
the money he has in the world, in stocks and loses it all.

Let us examine these choices and the possible alternatives to them one by one. It is likely that if he had not quit college he would have gone through it as thousands of others do and settled down to a humdrum, secure existence. It is possible, too, that he would have made much more money. What he chooses, instead, is something out of the ordinary. His persistence in the face of the adverse screen test at least involves risking failure. And once he is in Hollywood he again persists until he sees that he has no chance there. He goes to Hollywood out of a conviction; and if it is the conviction of an immature sophomore he also takes the consequences of acting out this conviction. When he returns home from California his rejection of the medical school is also based on a conviction. He will not go to medical school because, "I can't bear hospitals. Besides, I might make a mistake and hurt someone or even kill a patient. I couldn't stand that. Besides, I haven't got that sort of brains."[4]

His resignation from his salesman's job is again an assertion of his dignity as an individual. It is not that he has resigned in a huff only and if given the job back would take it. But the point is that against his father's and his wife's insistence, he would rather bide his time in the midst of retired people at Hotel Gloriana than submit himself to the humiliation of begging for what he threw away manfully. He thinks while speaking to his wife over the phone :

> He would be better off with Margaret again than he was today. This was what she wanted to make him feel, and she drove it home. 'Are you in misery?' she was saying. 'But you have deserved it.' And he could not return to her any more than he could beg Rojax to take him back. If it cost him his life, he could not. Margaret had ruined him with Olive. She hit him and hit him, beat him, battered him, wanted to beat the very life out of him.   (p. 123)

His decision to invest $ 700 despite his suspicions about Tamkin's integrity is again a well-considered decision. As he says he makes twenty decisions before acting out the wrong one :

After much thought and hesitation and debate he invari-
ably took the course he had rejected innumerable times.
Ten such decisions made up the history of his life. He
had decided that it would be a bad mistake to go to Hollywood, and then he went. He had made up his mind not
to marry his wife, but ran off and got married. He had
resolved not to invest money with Tamkin, and then had
given him a check. (p. 27)

These words might at first suggest that Tommy is simply an
indecisive and confused man who changes his mind far too
frequently to get anywhere; or even that he can struggle into
wisdom but is fool enough not to act on it. Such a reading
would be off the mark. The choice he really makes is the
one he acts out. If he takes a course after rejecting it innumerable times the one he takes is still his real choice. It
would be easy enough for the rationalists to argue that each
one of Tommy's choices is "irrational". The rationality or
irrationality of choices, however, is always determined in the
context of certain goals. So the rationalist can argue that
Tommy's choices are wrong for the goals he (the rationalist)
has. He can't say that they were wrong for Tommy when he
made them or are wrong for him now. And even rational
choices do not guarantee predictable results. In any case, in
the existentialist view there are no rational grounds for choices.
And although in many of one's choices one is governed by
criteria, the criteria one applies are themselves *chosen*.

The upshot of the choices Tommy has made is that he is
not a successful man. Not that he would have minded being
one but he is not obsessed with success or the money and the
prestige that go with it. When at the breakfast table in
the hotel his father boasts to a fellow guest that Tommy's
income is up in five figures, and Mr. Perls, the guest, eagerly
starts reckoning Tommy's income tax, Tommy thinks with
disgust: "UGH! How they love money. . . They adore money!
Holy money! Beautiful money! It was getting so that people
were feeble-minded about everything except money. While
if you didn't have it you were a dummy, a dummy! You had
to excuse yourself from the face of the earth. Chicken! That's
what it was. The world's business. If only he could find a

way out of it" (p. 41). Later, expressing what he has always
felt about his father, Tommy tells him: "No but you hate
me. And if I had money you wouldn't. By God, you have
to admit it. The money makes the difference. Then we would
be a fine father and son, if I was a credit to you—so you could
boast and brag about me all over the hotel. But I am not the
right type of son." And when his father says, "Carry nobody
on your back," Tommy answers : "Just keep your money.
Keep it and enjoy it yourself. That is the ticket" (p. 61).

Tommy needs money and would be grateful if he got it
from his father but what he needs and wants even more is
some sympathy—at least from where he thinks he can legitima-
tely expect it. As he tells his father, he really wants "assistance". After having discovered his losses in the stocks when
he goes to see his father, Dr. Adler chides him for trying his
patience. Tommy answers : "I try not to. But one word
from you, just a word, would go a long way. I've never asked
you for very much. But you are not a kind man, Father.
You don't give the little bit I beg you for" (p. 119). What
finally demonstrates Tommy's basic indifference to money,
despite his great need for it, is the fact that he very quickly
forgets that he is broke and gets involved with the funeral
crowd : "But within a few minutes he had forgotten Tamkin.
He stood along the wall with 'others and looked toward the
coffin and the slow line that was moving past it, gazing at the
face of the dead" (p. 126).

For Bellow Tommy's choices are perhaps not as admirable
as I have just suggested they are. Bellow clearly views
Tommy's decisions with sympathy but he also views them
with irony as a series of bunglings. Tommy himself is aware
that he has bungled. He is also aware that the responsibility
for it is his own and that others, even his father, are justified
in their contempt for his bunglings.

But what of the truth ? Ah, the truth was that there were
problems, and of these problems his father wanted no part.
His father was ashamed of him. The truth, Wilhelm
thought, was very awkward. He pressed his lips together,
and his tongue went soft; it pained him far at the back, in
the cords and throat, and a knot of ill formed in his chest.

Dad never was a pal to me when I was young, he reflected.
He was at the office or the hospital, or lecturing. He
expected me to look out for myself and never gave me
much thought. Now he looks down on me. And may
be in some respects he's right. (p. 18)

What is significant here is Tommy's awareness that the whole
question of truth bristles with problems, that the truth is awkward, as also his awareness that in coping with the problems
he has somehow not come out right.

But we should look at Tommy's decisions not simply as
Bellow looks at them but from the existentialist standpoint as
well. The existentialist attitude towards life involves, first,
an honest encounter with the facts of one's situation to the
extent such an encounter is possible. In other words, this
means the individual's willingness to constantly examine himself and his context. Such examination is always bound to yield
only a limited perception of the truth even in purely subjective
terms. What matters, though, is the individual's habit of examining himself. Tommy is not merely perceptive of his environment and shrewd at interpreting it but, as he shows in the
talent scout's office, he is aware of what is happening to himself
as well. When the agent classifies him in the image of just a
sympathetic human being and a good provider, he not only
instantly sees that he has been classified as a loser, he also
recognizes that "he had been not only confused but hurt" (p.
26). Next, the existentialist attitude involves doubt, uncertainty,
anguish and fear before the choice is made because there is no
reality except the subjective one, and one can only grope and
do one's best. Tommy goes through all this when he leaves
for Hollywood, aware of the risks: "Still, for three months
Wilhelm delayed his trip to California. He wanted to start
out with the blessings of his family, but they were never given.
He quarrelled with his parents and his sister. And then,
when he was best aware of the risks and knew a hundred
reasons against going and had made himself sick with fear, he
left home" (p. 27).

In California he takes a new name, Tommy—a change his
father would not accept. In the inexperience and inncocence
of youth he hopes the change of name would mean a change in

his self as well. It doesn't turn out that way. In retrospect
he reflects: " . . . there's really very little that a man can
change at will. He can't change his lungs, or nerves, or constitution or temperament. They're not under his control.
When he's young and strong and impulsive and dissatisfied
with the way things are he wants to rearrange them to assert
his freedom. He can't overthrow the government or be differently born; he only has a little scope and may be a foreboding,
too, that essentially you can't change. Nevertheless, he makes
a gesture and becomes Tommy Wilhelm" (p. 29). Yes, he has
always remained Wilky. Yet, he has made his gesture and
that is what counts. He has never felt like Tommy but it
doesn't matter. The existentialist way does not guarantee a
sure success in each attempt to identify one's true self—indeed
it is an almost endless search; failure in finding one's true
self is part of the whole enterprise of living. What is
striking in this reflection is not so much what critics have
called the failure of the pretender self to smother the real
self. Rather it is Tommy's gesture in taking on a new self
hoping it would change his identity for the better and,
even more important, his honest realization that he has failed
in his attempt. As he says, "Yes, it had been a stupid thing
to do, but it was his imperfect judgment at the age of twenty
which should be blamed. He had cast off his father's name,
and with it his father's opinion of him. It was, he knew it
was, his bid for liberty. Adler being in his mind the title of
the species, Tommy the freedom of the person. But Wilky
was his inescapable self" (p. 29). Tommy's integrity lies in his
facing what he perhaps mistakenly thinks was a mistake. He,
like anyone, must make a series of mistakes to get anywhere
near the discovery of his self and identity before he can make
something resembling a final choice. Starting at twenty he is
forty-four before he realises that the values Dr. Adler and
Tamkin represent in differing ways—concern for success and
money and for the here and now—are not his values any more.
Like Henderson his soul cries : "I want, I want," and what it
wants is certainly not "success," although he may often be led
by his material hardship and the resulting self-doubt and confusion into believing that he has flopped. His story not only
on that day but in the past too seems to be of a constant

struggle to find out what he wants and to *want* it even if later it turns out that he had wanted the wrong thing. ⌈In the existentialist view of the human individual, however, the only thing that makes a choice right is one's having made it oneself and one's willingness to take the responsibility for it.⌋ This is what makes Tommy superior to his successful father who has achieved worldly success without taking any "false steps". He simply has not dared to take any but the steps society and convention have prescribed for worldly success.

Tamkin, on the other hand, has daring but lacks integrity. Unconsciously, or perhaps consciously, he does help Tommy in his discovery of the self. The poem he gives Tommy carries much significance for him, even if he at first fails to see what it means and for whom. But Tamkin's chief interest here is in his representing a false value in his stress on the here and now.

For the existentialist the moment is significant. Choices lead to commitment and commitment is not for the moment only. Seizing the day in the literal sense is a betrayal of the self, and Tamkin with his shifting roles and selves has no self left to commit to anything. Tommy, on the other hand, does precisely the opposite. He refuses to seize the day in Tamkin's sense. In both hungering for sympathy and understanding and in giving it, first to the old man Rappapotos and finally in aligning himself with the dead stranger, he seizes the day by seizing the eternal.

The twentieth century view of man—particularly the western view—would appear to give the highest importance to the itegrity of the individual as the centre of ultimate value. The fundamental question for the individual therefore is, "Who am I?" Jerry H. Bryant in his book, *The Open Decision*, observes:

What we consider to be threats depends upon what we consider to be good and real—that is, the individual. If he is defined as an 'open decision,' a paradoxical consciousness responsible for his own self-creation from a wide range of alternatives around him, then the threats upon him will be those things that thwart the implementation of the 'open decision.' It is true that a good many of the problems arising from these threats as dealt with by our novelists involve a focus on introspection—false consciousness, for example, requires that one achieve a greater psychological openness in order to execute the 'open decision.'[5]

In our century the western mind no longer finds superhuman absolutes within man's grasp. The self therefore becomes the absolute for which man must search, and the unending process of the search makes consciousness the sovereign factor even when the consciousness may reveal its very limitations. Becoming conscious then is an essential part of the search for the self because it helps the individual become more himself as well as become aware of the obstacles to becoming himself.

In *Seize the Day* Bellow shows Tommy's consciousness in a state of perpetual activity either through recollection of the past and its critical analysis or through a scrutiny of the present. Disgusted by his father's whitewashing of his failure in the presence of another guest at the hotel, this is what Tommy thinks (and Bellow projects Tommy's consciousness through a very effective combination of the third person narrator with an almost stream-of-consciousness technique):

He was a little tired. The spirit, the peculiar burden of his existence lay upon him like an accretion, a load, a hump. In any moment of quiet, when sheer fatigue prevented him from struggling, he was apt to feel this mysterious weight, this growth or collection of nameless things which it was the business of his life to carry about. That must be what a man was for. This large, odd, excited, fleshy, blond, abrupt personality named Wilhelm, or Tommy, was here, present, in the present—Dr. Tamkin had been putting into his mind many suggestions about the present moment, the here and now—this Wilky, or Tommy Wilhelm, forty-four years old, father of two sons, at present living in the Hotel Gloriana, was assigned to be the carrier of a load which was his own self, his characteristic self. There was no figure or estimate for the value of this load. But it is probably exaggerated by the subject, T.W. Who is a visionary sort of animal. Who has to believe that he can know why he exists. Though he has never seriously tried to find out why. (p. 44)

The passage reveals at least three things. One, that Tommy feels defeated. Two, that at least partly his sense of defeat is aggravated by the disgust provoked in him by the false values causing his father to be hypocritical. Three, and most important, that Tommy is not merely conscious of his down at heel condition but of the burden that his characteristic self is. It is a very high degree of consciousness of one's self indeed. The very process in the consciousness that this passage warns us against is the last sentence: "But it is probably exaggerated by the subject, T.W. Who is a visionary sort of animal. Who has to believe that he can know why he exists. Though he has never seriously tried to find out why." The novel is rich in such moments showing Tommy's consciousness turned upon himself—and upon itself—in the very moment of its process.

Through the process of his consciousness he is moving closer to the moment when one's authentic self can be accessible. In moving towards a greater awareness of the self Tommy may not necessarily, indeed he does not, become conscious of what is happening to him. In other words, he may not be a theoriser on the change he is undergoing. This becomes evident in his response to the pompous—and bad—poem Tamkin gives him. The poem is entitled "MECHANISM VS FUNCTIONALISM: ISM VS HISM" :

> If thee thyself couldst only see
> Thy greatness that is and yet to be,
> Thou would feel joy-beauty-what ecstasy.
> They are at thy feet, earth-moon-sea, the trinity.
>
> Why-forth then dost thou tarry
> And partake thee only of the crust
> And skim the earth's surface narry
> When all creations art thy just?
>
> Seek ye then that which art not there
> In thine own glory let thyself rest.
> Witness. Thy power is not bare.
> Thou art King. Thou art at thy best.
>
> Look then right before thee.
> Open thine eyes and see.
> At the foot of Mt. Serenity
> Is thy cradle to eternity. (p. 82)

In what is almost low comedy Tommy responds to the poem like an idiot in the presence of "Mona Lisa." He cannot make head or tail of the poem but, ironically, suspects that Tamkin is illiterate enough to give importance to such nonsense. The point Bellow may be making here is that whereas Tamkin is the incorrigible theoriser, as his habitual discourses with Tommy show, Tommy is the one who is living reality out. Tamkin can facilely swear by man being the crown of creation. Such a view, however, is unrecognisably out of context in modern times and therefore can make no sense at all to Tommy even though he is not exactly a genius. On the other hand, what Tommy knows of man is that his life is a long struggle to identify his self through what he himself calls an endless series of mistakes. These mistakes, the defeat, the restlessness, the anguish, are all inevitably part of the search.

NOTES

1. Saul Bellow, "Distractions of a Fiction Writer," in *The Living Novel : A Symposium*, ed. Granville Hicks (New York: Macmillan, 1957), p. 15.
2. Abraham Kaplan, "The Second Fall of Man," *Salmagundi*, No. 30 (Summer 1975), pp. 67-68.
3. Patrick Morrow, "Threat and Accommodation : The Novels of Saul Bellow," *Midwest Quarterly*, 8, No. 4 (Summer 1967), pp. 392-93.
4. Saul Bellow, *Seize the Day* (New York : Avon Books, 1977), p. 20. All subsequent references to the novel are from this edition and are incorporated in the essay in parentheses.
5. Jerry H. Bryant, *The Open Decision* (New York: The Free Press, 1970), p. 284.

9

RICHARD WRIGHT'S *THE OUTSIDER* : EXISTENTIALIST EXEMPLAR OR CRITIQUE?

Amritjit Singh

THE OUTSIDER (1953) is one of the first consciously existentialist novels written by an American. Richard Wright had been living in Paris for a few years and had not published any book since his autobiography, *Black Boy* (1945). *The Outsider* was his first major work of fiction since *Native Son* (1940), which had received much critical attention and also caused considerable controversy. Wright had started working on *The Outsider* as early as 1947, hoping to make it a "great book," a book, to use his own words, "one can read feeling the movement and rhythm of a man alive and confronting the world with all its strength."[1] In this book, he would deal with the concept of freedom and he decided to familiarize himself with existentialism as part of his preparation. As he learned more about existentialist thought, he felt that it corresponded to his own vision of life and human responsibility. During this period, Wright was, however, exposed to many other influences too. One of his deeply-felt concerns at this time was the impact of industrialisation on the modern world, especially in Asia and Africa. The Cold War between the East and the West was serious enough, but a deeper problem to Wright was "the total extinction of the concept of a human being which has prevailed for 2000 years," bringing in the worst features of the consumer society.[2] *The Outsider* had its origin, thus, in Wright's attempt to resolve the dilemma of the individual *versus* society, the mind *versus* materialism.

Wright's view of existentialism was shaped primarily

through his responses to Sartre, and it is no coincidence that the two men came to place similar faith in violence in the context of colonialism. Wright's responses were regulated to a great extent by Dorothy Norman who introduced him to existentialism and the writings of Kierkegaard, Nietzsche and Heidegger. And it was at her place that he first met Sartre during the latter's visit to the United States in 1946. Later, he met Camus, Sartre and Simone de Beauvoir in Paris and admired Camus greatly until Camus sided with the French Colonists in the Algerian War. Simone de Beauvoir was more accessible than Sartre and became a closer friend of the Wrights, but French existentialism for Wright was represented primarily by Sartre. Wright and Sartre worked well together on political issues because of their shared Marxist sympathies. Wright was surprised and delighted that Sartre saw a connection between his experience of oppression, the Nazi occupation of France, and that of all oppressed and colonised peoples. The two had, however, arrived at their positions from different directions. As Michel Fabre points out, "since his rupture with the Communist Party, Wright had been a humanist in both ethics and politics, but while he had evolved from politics to morality, Sartre had proceeded from morality to politics."[3] Both believed in committed action and while Wright's works used violence consistently as a mode of self-expression, Sartre saw it as an unavoidable tool in the hands of the oppressed in their war of liberation against the colonists. In his 1961 Preface to Frantz Fanon's *The Wretched of the Earth*, Sartre makes a frontal attack on Western apathy and complacency towards the Third World. Most Westerners, according to Sartre, felt they were innocent of the crimes of colonialism because they were not settlers or colonizers themselves. Sartre charges all Westerners with complicity through silence in order to arouse their sense of shame and guilt. Shame, for both Marx and Sartre, is a revolutionary sentiment. Sartre warned that violence by the colonizers will be returned by violence from the colonized; "for violence, like Achilles' lance, can heal the wound it has inflicted."[4] According to Sartre, "to shoot down a European is to kill two birds with one stone, to destroy an oppressor and the man he oppresses at the same time; there remain a dead man and a free man; the survivor, for the

first time feels a *national* soil under his feet."[5] Wright's use of
violence in *The Outsider* does not, of course, owe itself entirely
to existentialist vindications of violence. Violence is endemic
to the black American situation; just as to cite the bare facts
of black American life is to make an anti-American document,
to protest these facts is to incite or invite violence.

The Outsider is no more than a murder mystery if we concern ourselves with the plot in its bare outline. But Wright
leaves no doubt in our minds that he intends it to be a serious
philosophical work, a novel of ideas. Unlike his earlier work,
The Outsider is not tied to a realistic sociological portrayal of
black American life. The protagonist Crass Damon is not
merely a black man—he is a thinking, questioning man facing
the complexities of twentieth-century life.[6] But, as in *Native
Son*, Wright resorts to some transparent devices to build up
the intellectual content of his story. The long essay that
becomes part of the extended conversation between Damon
and Ely Houston, the New York District Attorney, permits
Wright, through Damon, to spell out some of his own ideas on
modern man and industrialisation, religion and capitalism.
In a review, Max Eastman had described the device with some
justification as "an ingenious way to compel a lazy-minded
nation to read an essay," and also accused Wright of "passing
from the Communist conspiracy to the Existentialist racket."[7]

The Outsider is the story of Cross Damon, whose name
brings together the Christian ethic of suffering and a Nietzschean demonism.[8] As the novel opens, we find Cross drinking
compulsively against protests from his friends and co-workers
at the post-office where he works in an environment reminiscent
of Bartleby's Wall Street office desk. Cross wants to drown
the worries that stem from the demands of a separated wife,
Gladys, and three children. The situation is complicated now
by his involvement with a fifteen-year old girl, Dot. Dot, pregnant by Cross, is getting ready to exploit the situation to her
own advantage. Dot wants Cross to marry her, which he cannot
because Gladys refuses to release him in a divorce—or else, she
would initiate legal proceedings against Damon for assault and
rape. Damon's mother, whose Christian ethic he would like to
negate if possible, is in a state of shock at these new develop-
ments and urges Cross to find a solution and act quickly.

The gripping tale of Damon's career is divided into five sections: Dread, Dream, Descent, Despair, Decision, the sixth D—"Death"—permeating all the sections. The story moves with remarkable speed, creating a suspension of disbelief in the reader with regard to its many contradictions and implausibilities. The aloofness and the isolation of Cross from all around him are stressed in the early pages of the novel. Cross would like to open up and relax with someone, and to communicate, but "there was not a single man to whom he cared to confess the nightmare that was his life. He had sharp need of a confidant, and yet he knew that if he had an ideal confidant, before whom he could lay his whole story, he would have instantly regretted it, would have murdered his confidant the moment after he had confided to him his shame."[9] In Dostoevskian passages such as these, Wright tries to make Cross Damon a convincing character—someone who is separated from his friends and family by his pride, his highstrung nature and bewildered sensibility. But for these elements in his portrayal in the early pages, Cross of the later sections may be a completely implausible character, likely to appear like a man who has serious problems on hand, but not entirely unique or tough enough to be the dreaded desperado that he later becomes.

Cross wonders aloud: "Why were some people, fated, like Job, to live a never-ending debate between themselves and their sense of what they believed life should be? Why did some hearts feel insulted at being alive, humiliated at the terms of existence?" (p. 19) And just as Hawthorne's black-veiled priest senses sin and guilt in others, Cross develops a special intuitive sense of identifying 'outsiders'. He spots other 'outsiders'—people who feel a wall of separation between themselves and the surrounding society because of one reason or the other—prostitutes, Communists, women and non-whites in general, or a hunchback such as the District Attorney, Ely Houston, whom he meets later on a train journey to New York. He has a keen understanding of the murderous self-hatred that rules the lives of most black Americans and has a clear focus on the problems of modern life and the black man's place in it. Cross's antenna-like sensitivity to all 'outsiders' highlights the depth of his alienation and also indicates that it is a social malaise and not a psychic imbalance. The sense of wholeness that Cross appears to have lost defines a situation that is existentialist to the core. The need to authenticate oneself in a stultifying environment leads to an undying craving for freedom.

The plot deliberately dramatizes the existentialist theme of freedom. While Cross is still puzzling his way through the latest mess he has brought upon himself, Gladys has already made sure that she gets a fair share of the blackmail booty. She forces Cross to sign the house and the car over to her and demands that he borrow eight hundred dollars from the Postal Union to clear the titles of both. It is when he is returning with this money from the post-office that he stumbles upon an irresistible opportunity to start his life all over again. He is involved in a subway accident which he survives only to learn later from a radio announcement that he is officially dead because he has been mistaken for another fellow passenger. Harassed as he is by his many problems, he jumps at this chance to create a new existence, a new person out of his disposable past: "What was his past if he wanted to become another person? . . . Now, his past would have to be a deliberately constructed thing. . . . Others took their lives for grant-ed, he would have to mould his with a conscious aim. Why not? Was he not free to do so? That all men were free was the fondest and deepest conviction of his life. . . . He would do with himself what he would, what he liked" (p. 87).

In existentialist terms, there could not be a greater possi-bility than to have the freedom to act without limitation of any kind. Cross has the freedom to exercise a most funda-mental choice, causing him to experience what Kierkegaard describes as "the dizziness of freedom, what occurs when free-dom looks down into its own possibility."[10] But Cross, like an existentialist, insists on action, for only in action does existence attain concreteness and fullness. In his *Journals*, Kierkegaard has the following to say:

What I really lack is to be clear in my mind *what I am to do*. . . What good would it be to me to be able to develop a theory of the state and combine all the details into a single whole, and so construct a world in which I did not live, but only held up to the view of others![11]

And action for the existentialist is not mere function or mere activism; action properly so-called is intensely personal; it involves the whole man. Action implies freedom. Both Camus and Sartre, who influenced Wright at different times in different ways, are apostles of freedom. For Sartre as for Kierkegaard, freedom and existence are indistinguishable. But freedom itself is an ambiguous phenomenon. It is ambiguous because freedom is often taken to afford possibility, but possibility is to be considered as the opposite of "facticity." Facticity limits and defines possibility, since possibilities exist not in a vacuum but in actual situations. Cross was free to act but he could not exchange his existence for the existence of another. As Martin Heidegger puts it, man is 'thrown' into his situation. By changing one's name or exchanging one's situation this 'thrown-ness' (*Geworfenheit*) cannot be obliterated.[12] And nowhere is this ambiguity of freedom better revealed than in the action of *The Outsider*. It is a compound irony of Wright's plot and theme that Cross's choice involves the whole man in a perverted, macabre way—it involves remaking the man himself. In existentialist terms, Cross's unlimited possibility is perhaps more "Good God, man is free!" than "Hurrah, man is free!" The rare possibility that is afforded to Cross has only paved the way for a desultory fragmentary existence.

To give himself time to think out his strategy and to make sure all goes well at and after his supposed funeral, Cross checks into a cheap hotel where he runs into his old friend, Joe Thomas. Afraid that his plans to flee his past might be betrayed, he kills Joe and takes the train to New York in search of a new life, a new meaning for his re-created existence:

He was empty, face to face with a sense of dread more intense than anything he had ever felt before. He was alone. . . . Nothing made meaning; his life seemed to have turned into a static dream whose frozen images would remain unchanged throughout eternity. (p. 101)

This aloneness, this existentialist alienation remains with Cross to the end of his days. Existentially, man is alienated from his own deepest being, he is not himself but simply a cipher in the mass existence of the crowd, a cog in the modern industrial world.[13] Each person has to make decisions in his own unique situation and accept responsibility for these decisions.[14] Cross's total aloneness is underscored throughout the novel.

On the train to New York, Cross meets Bob Hunter, a West Indian waiter in the train restaurant and also strikes up a conversation with a Catholic priest and his friend who turns out to be Ely Houston, the hunchbacked District Attorney from New York City. Cross's fear of discovery permits Wright to introduce some Dostoevskian notes: "Was he being followed on this train? Wasn't this waiter being especially friendly to allay any fears he might have that he was being watched? Hadn't that waiter cursed the white folks with the idea of inducing in him a false notion of security?" (p. 122). Houston's hunchback, like Cross's own racial and intellectual isolation, serves the District Attorney well in empathising with the outsiders, the outcasts. He has a DuBois-like sense of the Negro's two-ness and claims that "this damned hump has given me more psychological knowledge than all the books I read at the university." (p. 133). Here and elsewhere in the novel, Wright uses dialogue to ensure that his themes and motifs are not missed. In speaking to Houston, Cross expounds his theory of man, which finds a sympathetic chord within Houston:

"Maybe man is nothing in particular," Cross said gropingly. "Maybe that's the terror of it. Man may be just anything at all. . . . And every move he makes, couldn't these moves be just to hide this awful fact? To twist it into something which he feels would make him rest and breathe a little easier? What man is is perhaps too much to be borne by man. . . ." (pp. 135-6)

On arrival in New York, Cross takes steps to give himself a new name and identity—Lionel Lane, the name of a man who had just been buried in the neighbourhood graveyard. He manages to procure Lane's duplicate birth certificate and draft card to close his tracks against possible discovery before he contacts Bob Hunter. Hunter has lost his job as waiter and has just joined the Communist Party to organise the workers. He introduces Cross to Gil and Eva Blount who would like to use Cross to dramatize discrimination against blacks in housing. Cross moves into the apartment of the Blounts and soon discovers that the Party has tricked Eva, a non-objective painter with inherited wealth, into marrying Gil, in order to keep her and her wealth within the Party. Cross and Eva are attracted to each other as victims of deception. Soon, Blount's neo-fascist landlord, Herndon, discovers Cross in the building. Later in the evening, the confrontation between Blount and Herndon leads to violence wherein Cross kills both. For Cross both were insects, one a neo-fascist and the other a condescending totalitarian. He had earlier killed Joe Thomas for purely practical reasons but his killing of Herndon and Blount was a conscious choice. Like Bigger Thomas, Cross too must exercise his existentialist choices, must express himself through deadly violence: "The universe seemed to be rushing at him with all its totality. He was anchored once again in life, in the flow of things; the world glowed with an intensity so sharp it made his body ache. . . . He knew exactly what he had done; he had done it deliberately, even though he had not planned it" (p. 227).

He manages to cover the clues that might expose his complicity, depending on the police to believe the strong possibility of Herndon and Blount killing each other. Cross hopes to discover some meaning in his life through his genuine love for Eva which she reciprocates to meet her own needs. But the implications of his actions trouble him: "As Hilton and Gil had acted toward Bob, so had he acted toward Gil and Herndon; he had assumed the role of policeman, judge, supreme court, and executioner—all in one swift and terrible moment. But if he resented their being little gods, how could he do the same?" (p. 230). When the medical examiner comes up with the theory that a third man may have murdered both Herndon and Blount, both Houston and Cross describe such a man in frightening terms. For Houston, such a man is "a bleak and tragic man. He is the twentieth century writ small." Cross concurs that for such a person, "all ethical laws are suspended. He acts like a God" (p. 283).

But Cross cannot stop with these murders alone. Finding

that John Hilton, a Party man, had betrayed Bob Hunter to
the Immigration authorities, Cross decides to kill Hilton too.
By this time, both the police and the Party have focussed on
him as a suspect. Houston confronts Cross with his discarded
identity but in the absence of definitive evidence, leaves him to
his own punishment:

> "Listen, Damon, you made your own law," Houston pro-
> nounced. "And, by God, I, for one, am going to let you
> live by it. I'm pretty certain you're finished with this kill-
> ing phase. . . . So, I'm going to let you go. See? yes; just
> go! *You're free*! Just like that." Houston snapped his fingers
> in Cross's face. "I'm going to let you keep this in your
> heart until the end of your days! . . . You are going to
> punish yourself, see? You are your own law, so you'll be
> your own judge. . . ." (pp. 429-30).

But Houston lets Damon go only after he has confronted him
with his own reality. Houston, Cross's "double" in the book,
lays him bare in a clear and strong description of Cross's
primum mobile, the desire to be a god among his fellow human
beings: "Desire is the mad thing, the irrational thing. Damon,
you peeled off layer after layer of illusion and make-believe
and stripped yourself down to just simply naked desire and you
thought that you had gotten hold of the core of reality. And,
in a sense, you had. But what does one do with desire? Man
desires ultimately to be a god" (p. 415).

Some of the animus directed against Communists in the
final pages of *The Outsider* has to do with Wright's own
experiences with the Party. To some extent, Wright felt close
to existentialism because he had come to distrust all forms of
authoritarianism. Communism, for him, denies individualism
and subjectivity. He charges that the driving force behind Communism is nothing but a lust for naked power:

> to hold absolute power over others, to define what they
>   hould love or fear, to decide if they were to live or die
> and thereby to ravage the whole of their beings—that was
> a sensuality that made sexual passion look pale by com-
> parison. It was a non-economic conception of existence.
> (p. 198)

While Bob Hunter's experienes in *The Outsider* were based on the actual case of Hank Johnson, it bears many parallels to the case of Ross Washington, a black Party member, that Wright had described at length in his essay included in *The God That Failed* (ed. Richard Crossman), and is now also available in *American Hunger*, his second autobiography. Both in *American Hunger* and *The Outsider*, Wright underscores the Communist Party's distrust of intellectuals: "the slightest sign of any independence of thought or feeling, even if it aided the party in its work, was enough to make one suspect, to brand one as a dangerous traitor."[15] This denunciation of Communism links up with the larger theme of *The Outsider*, the tyranny by which one may arbitrarily decide to play the role of God and control the destiny of others.

Wright's handling of the story's ending is perhaps an indication of his deep distrust of the Party's tyranny. While the dispenser of law, Ely Houston, leaves Cross alone to devise his own form of punishment, the Party folks are not prepared to let him go scot free. They must settle seores blatantly and immediately, leaving little room for psychological retribution or recoupment. Two Party men shadow Cross and finally shoot him down. The final scene, reminiscent in many ways of Bigger Thomas's last meeting with Max, introduces a surprising new element into the conversation between Cross and Houston:

> "Nothing . . ." He lay very still and summoned all of his strength. "The search can't be done alone." He let his voice issue from a dry throat in which he felt death lurking. "Never alone. . . . Alone a man is nothing. . . . *Man is a promise that he must never break. . . .*"

> "Is there anything, Damon, you want me to tell anybody?" His mind reeled at the question. There was so much and yet it was so little. . . .

> "I wish I ha some way to give the meaning of my life to others. . . . To make a bridge from man to man . . . Starting from scratch every time is . . . is no good. Tell them not to come down this road. . . . Men hate themselves and it makes them hate others. . . . *We must find, some way of*

being good to ourselves . . . *Man is all we've got.* . . . I
wish I could ask men to meet themselves. . . . We're
strangers to ourselves." He was silent for a moment, then
he continued, whispering: "Don't think I'm so odd and
strange. . . . I'm not. . . . I'm legion. . . . I've lived alone,
but I'm everywhere. . . . Man is returning to the earth.
. . . For a long time he had been sleeping, wrapped in a
dream. . . . (pp. 439-40; italics mine).

This final scene is also an important clue to our interpretation of the novel. Is the novel to be seen primarily as a
dramatisation of an existentialist thesis, or, is Wright rejecting
existentialist philosophy as indequate to cope with the problems
of the modern world? Or, is *The Outsider* perhaps a kind of
cathartic exercise, Wright's attempt to purge himself of
existentialist attitudes and stances? Growing anxious about his
existence, Cross seizes upon an opportunity to foreclose his
original identity and although he is trapped in the process, he
appears to have gained an insight into the human situation.
He is urged by the Party to be a non-entity and he treats
others in the same way; only in death does he gain a semblance
of wholeness. Inasmuch as *The Outsider* dramatizes the
dilemma of its protagonist, death sets a boundary to everything
and Cross in shown to perceive a unity of existence.
    There remains a doubt in the reader's mind, however,
about the authenticity of Cross's ultimate assertions about
man and life. Internal and external evidence suggests that
Wright had written the novel to work out the implications of
an existentialist stance, as a conscious stock-taking point in his
own intellectual, spiritual and aesthetic development. The book
undoubtedly has the mechanical obviousness of a dogma being
rehearsed for possible adoption and lacks the vitality and
appeal of *Native Son*, where, partly because of Wright's close-
ness to the concrete facts of Afro-American existence, one gets
the feel of experience lived through, felt on the pulse. To describe Wright's earlier works like *Black Boy* and *Native Son* as
existentialist would be to introduce unnecessary semantic confusion into our discussions, but it seems reasonable to suggest
that there were enough indications in his earlier work—e.g.,
his attitude to God in *Black Boy*, Bigger's half-articulate new

sense of himself in the last scene of *Native Son*, and the wide-
ranging, non-racial implications of a story like "The Man Who
Lived Underground"—to suggest his subsequent gravitation
towards the philosophical literature of the alienated and self-
determining man.

It would seem unlikely that the novelist in Wright would
have stopped with a Nietzschean existentialism. But if we
lay aside all that Wright rejects in the pages of *The Outsider*,
we are left with little that affirms or lends hope. As Orville
Prescott noted in an early review, one may assume that Wright
deplores "Cross' moral weakness and irrational behaviour, but
that he finds much cogency in Cross' philosophy. That men
as brilliant as Richard Wright feel this way is one of the
symptoms of the intellectual and moral crisis of our times."[16]
For a few years before he wrote *The Outsider*, Wright had
been drawn to causes on behalf of colonized nations in Africa
and Asia. Fabre tells us that in the early fifties, Wright had
been removing himself each day "from purely American preoccupations by acquiring a more European, more global view
of his own situation in particular, of the black situation in
general, and the situation of contemporary man."[17] Wright's
unpublished article, "I Choose Exile" (1950), had strongly
emphasized the need for Americans to break away from narrow
provincialism and to inject a Third-World awareness into a
renewed pursuit of the highest American ideals. Is it possible,
then, that Wright the political activist cherished goals and
sought solutions which clashed with his overwhelming condi-
tioning as a Western intellectual, and a very American indivi-
dualist?[18] Wright's quest for a new humanism remained
unfulfilled, possibly because as an artist he could not integrate
his newly-discovered Third-World awareness with his pre-
dominantly Western orientation. This inner dichotomy of
Wright's is perhaps responsible for the ambivalence that the
reader experiences in responding to *The Outsider* as an
existentialist novel.

NOTES

1. Quoted in Michel Fabre, *The Unfinished Quest of Richard Wright* (New York : William Morrow, 1973), p. 315.
2. Ibid., p. 326.
3. Ibid., p. 322.
4. Preface to Frantz Fannon, *The Wretched of the Earth* trans. Constance Farrington (New York: Grove, 1968), p. 22.
5. Ibid., p. 22.
6. Cf. Lorraine Hansberry's review, *Freedom* 14 (April 1953), p. 7: "Cross Damon is someone you will never meet on the Southside of Chicago or in Harlem. For if he is anything at all, he is the symbol of Wright's new philosophy—the glorification of—nothingness."
7. Max Eastman, "Man as a Promise," *Freeman*, 3 (May 4, 1953), 567-68.
8. Fabre, p. 366.
9. Richard Wright, *The Outsider* (New York: Harper and Row, 1953), p. 14. All subsequent quotations from the novel are from this edition and have been cited in the text.
10. John Macquarrie, *Existentialism* (1972; Harmondsworth: Penguin, 1973), p. 54.
11. Ibid., p. 175.
12. Ibid., p. 191. A little earlier (p. 190), John Macquarrie defines facticity thus: "I cannot exchange my existence for the existence of another. I am I . . . . I just happen to be this particular person and no other. I have this particular body; I am of this particular race and colour; I have this particular intelligence quotient, this particular emotional make-up, and so on. Furthermore, I have been born into this particular historical situation in this particular society, and all kinds of forces are operating in the situation and in the society to shape my life and to limit what I can become."
13. Ibid., p. 204.
14. Ibid., p. 103.
15. Richard Wright, *American Hunger*. Afterword by Michel Fabre. (New York: Harper and Row, 1977), p. 120.
16. *New York Times* (March 18, 1953), p. 29. Quoted in John M. Reilly, ed., *Richard Wright: The Critical Reception* (New York: Burt Franklin, 1978), p. 194.
17. Fabre, p. 316.
18. For a stimulating discussion of Wright's dichotomous attitude toward the West (or for that matter, toward individualism), see Nina Kressner Cobb, "Richard Wright : Individualism Reconsidered." *CLA Journal*, 21, No. 3 (March 1978), p. 335-54. Cobb too points to "signs of discomfort" in the conclusions of both *Native Son* and *The Outsider*.

10

WALKER PERCY: *THE MOVIEGOER*

Jacob Sloan

WALKER Percy is the most explicitly existentialist of American novelists. This is not to say that his novels are tractarian harangues by any means; they are fictions first and foremost. Their characters are lively and credible, sharply differentiated from one another, and the action flows from their vicissitudes, not from a predetermined author's schema of plot. The manners and morals of Percy's world in *The Moviegoer*—New Orleans, Louisiana, in the late 1950s—are carefully and shrewdly reported. Percy is a writer who has no need of Henry James's injunction: "Be one of those on whom nothing is lost". Nothing is lost on the author of *The Moviegoer*—no nuance of gesture or speech, or detail of the furniture of daily life. Finally, the vantage point from which the author writes is identical with that of his hero: both play the classical role of participant-observer made familiar to us by modern anthropology. There is no *deus ex machina in The Moviegoer* to solve with its surprise appearance the unresolvable dilemmas of the work; the author offers no easy solutions.

Yet *The Moviegoer* is definitely a novel of ideas, and the ideas are existentialist; existentialist terms are sprinkled throughout the novel; there is even a direct reference to Kierkegaard in the body of the novel to complement the Kierkegaard quotation at its head.

This is an existentialist novel by deliberation. Percy came to it after writing some thirteen serious essays—religious-psycho-logical-linguistic-socio-politico—philosophical meditations that were printed in religious, technical and high -brow journals like *Commonweal* and *Partisan Review* and *Psychiatry* (a medical man by training and profession, Percy has been under treatment, has practiced psychiatry and has taught it at Tulane University). His essays were brilliant, penetrating, and original, and were well regarded in intellectual circles. But Percy had been converted to Roman Catholicism; in the late 1950s he turned to the novel form in order to bring his "message"—the message of Christian existentialism—closer to the lives of the ordinary people he was writing about and for.

The Moviegoer was published in 1961, after Percy had made two false starts—novels that were too wordy, too preachy, too obvious. He quickly learned from these failures; *The Moviegoer* won the highly regarded National Book Award, and is now considered a minor modern classic. His prime exponent has been Robert Coles, the social psychiatrist. Coles's sympathetic and insightful *Walker Percy, an American Search* is an invaluable introduction to Percy's ideas, essays, and novels set against the background of his life and the thinkers and novelists who have influenced him. The index to the Coles book reads like a catalogue of the existentialist movement; besides the inevitable Kierkegaard and Heidegger, there is Jacques Maritain, Franz Kafka, W.H. Auden, George Bernanos, Flannery O'Connor, and of course, Martin Buber, Albert Camus and Jean-Paul Sartre. There is also Suzanne Langer for the Greek philosophical background, together with Thomas Aquinas and Augustine for the classical church position. Perhaps not too surprisingly, considering Percy's psychological and linguistic preoccupations, there is the interpersonalist psychiatrist Harry Stack Sullivan and the structural linguist Noam Chomsky, some of whose findings Coles feels that Percy anticipated.

Like Saul Bellow alone among contemporary American novelists, Walker Percy is an intellectual novelist. Where Bellow's ideas revolve around romanticism, Percy's revolve around existentialism. Where Bellow writes from an intellectual tradition deriving from the Jewish experience, Percy writes from the tradition and experience of catholic Christianity. The writings of both novelists are enriched by their sense of history—a sense so missing in contemporary American

novelists like Barthelme, Vonnegut, Pynchon, with their para-
noid reconstruction of our times as a terrible mutant unrelated
to the history of mankind.

But there is a significant difference between Bellow and
Percy: Bellow is a typical post-18th century Enlightenment
secular Jew who identifies with the Jewish historic experience
but not with its religious elements. (He has commented
casually that he has never been inclined to step into a library
to "read" the Talmud). But Percy does not suffer from
Bellow's religious hang-ups. To the contrary, his religion is
the spur to his intellectual activity, and to his work as a
novelist.

Percy has clearly and directly described the role that he
expects a novelist to play in his essay, "Notes for a Novel":

> The novelist writes about the coming end in order to warn
> about present ills and so avert the end . . . The wounded
> man has a better view of the battle than those still shooting.
> The novelist is less like a prophet than he is like the canary
> that coal miners used to take down the shaft to test the air.
> When the canary gets unhappy, utters plaintive cries, and
> collapses, it may be time for the miners to surface and
> think things over.

Here, the two chief elements of Percy's writings are immediately evident: the evangelical end, or message, and the
metaphorical means. Actually, throughout *The Moviegoer*, the
two are closely linked. The same metaphor of the wounded
soldier who gains sudden insight into reality reappears in *The
Moviegoer* and is associated with other metaphors in which an
accident assumes special meaning.

The hero of *The Moviegoer*, Binx Bolling—the "I" of the
novel—tells us that he began his "search" for the meaning of
his life in 1951. He was a soldier in Korea, and one day he
found himself lying on the ground injured. His shoulder was
"pressed hard against the ground," as if somebody were sitting
on him. He did not think about his situation, though. He
stared at a dung beetle six inches away. As he watched that
beetle he felt himself "on to something." If he got out of the
fix he was in, he told himself, he would "pursue the search."

Exactly what happened to Binx in Korea in 1951? He does not know for sure; but we know, from reading Percy's essays and Kierkegaard, that Binx became—and still is—the wounded man who has a better view of the battle than those still shooting—than the rest of us in this confused world.

Nor is Binx alone. Kate, his disturbed cousin with whom he shares a secret understanding of the inconsequentiality of everyday life, had a similar experience—she too has been in an accident, which killed her fiancé but from which she emerged unhurt. But she is still confused as to the meaning of that miraculous, transcendent experience. She confuses it with the conventional illusion of heroism as Binx does not.

> (Binx) "Your mother thought it was the accident that still bothered you."
> (Kate) "Did you expect me to tell her otherwise?"
> "That it did not bother you?"
> "That it gave me life. That's my secret, just as the war is your secret."
> "I did not like the war,"
> "Because afterward everyone said: What a frightful experience she went through and doesn't she do remarkably well. So then I did very well indeed. I would have made a good soldier."
> "Why do you want to be a soldier?"
> "How simple it would be to fight. What a pleasant thing it must be to be among people who are afraid for the first time when you yourself for the first time in your life have a proper flesh-and-blood enemy to be afraid of. What a lark! Isn't that the secret of heroes?"
> "I couldn't say. I wasn't a hero."

The novelist he has in mind, says Percy (like the non-hero, not anti-hero, of *The Moviegoer*) is no hero: "I locate him not on a scale of merit—he is not necessarily a good novelist—but in terms of goals. He is . . . a writer who has an explicit and ultimate concern with the nature of man and the nature of reality where man finds himself." Paul Tillich has made the phrase "ultimate concern" a key concept in his theological thinking. "Where man finds himself" has a Germanic ring—

it is a Buberian turn of phrase, since naturalized in American existentialist writing.

Percy goes on to offer an accurate description of the existentialist novelist's *modus operandi*:

> Instead of constructing a plot and creating a cast of characters from a world familiar to everybody, he is more apt to set forth with a stranger in a strange land where the signposts are enigmatic but which he sets out to explore nevertheless.

This is very familiar. Percy does not pretend to originality. He classes this sort of novelist with whom he obviously wishes to be identified with "writers as diverse as Dostoevsky, Tolstoy, Camus, Faulkner, Flannery O'Connor and Sartre".

Percy has excluded English writers from his list. He explains why with his usual serious wit:

> The nineteenth century Russian novelists were haunted by God; many of the French existentialists are haunted by his absence. The English novelist is not much interested one way or another. The English novel traditionally takes place in a society as everyone sees it and takes it for granted. If there are vicars and churches prominent in the society, there will be vicars and churches in the novel. If not, not. So much for vicars and churches.

The stranger whom Percy's ideal novelist places in a strange land is straight out of the existentialist canon—he is Camus' *L'Etranger* all over again. But not entirely. For there is a considerable difference between Camus' Meersault and Percy's Binx of *The Moviegoer*—perhaps "distance" is a better word than "difference". There is an extra distance separating the stranger Binx from the strange land he has wandered into. Characteristically, Percy translates that extra distance into the plot of a movie that Binx, the inveterate moviegoer goes to see. Binx tells us about it:

> The movie was about a man who lost his memory in an accident and as a result lost everything; his friends, his family

his money. He found himself a stranger in a strange city. Here he had to make a fresh start, find a new place to live, a new girl. It was supposed to be a tragedy, his losing all this, and he seemed to suffer a great deal. On the other hand, things were not so bad after all. In no time he found a very picturesque place to live, a houseboat on the river, and a very handsome girl, the local librarian.

Here is the existential statement in a movie metaphor. The problem with modern existence is that we do not know that our lives are inauthentic, that we are strangers in a strange world, that we are suffering.

Percy's tone is close to that of Kafka among the existentialist novelists in its dry, matter-of-fact, tongue-in-cheek humour with a grave undercurrent of persistent despair. Percy's touch is equally light and equally devastating, as he notes the masks which human beings assume to defend themselves against the realization of their inauthenticity, their alienation, what he calls the "everydayness" of the modern age. But Percy is at the same time deeply compassionate. Here is his cool, yet sympathetic description of how Mercer, his aunt's black butler, sees himself:

I know for a fact that Mercer steals regularly from (Binx's) aunt by getting kickbacks from the servants and tradespeople. But you can't call him a thief and let it go at that. Mercer has aspirations.

How does he see himself? When he succeeds in seeing himself, it is as a remarkable sort of fellow, a man who keeps himself well-informed in science and politics. This is why I am always uneasy when I talk to him. I hate it when his vision of himself dissolves and he sees himself as neither, neither old retainer nor expert in current events. Then his eyes get muddy and his face runs together behind his mustache . . . . On his bed lay a well-thumbed volume put out by the Rosicrucians called *How to Harness Your Secret Powers.* The poor bastard.

There is in this passage more than a hint of condescension toward Mercer, both as a black man and as a servant. This

condescension is inevitable in a middle-class twenty-nine year
old stockbroker in the Southern city of New Orleans, where
racist feeling ran high in the late 1950s, reawakened by the
1954 U.S. Supreme Court decision outlawing segregation in
education. Percy wrote in *Commonweal*, in 1956, that, "the
traditional world view of the upper class white Southerer"
was no longer "adequate to the situation".

But Binx is equally amused by his aunt's intellectual pre-
tensions, her pose of urbane stoicism:

> Scattered over the satinwood table is the usual litter of
> quarterlies and roughpaper weeklies and, as always, the
> great folio of *The Life of the Buddha*. My aunt likes to
> say she is an Episcopalian by emotion, a Greek by nature
> and a Buddhist by choice.

Binx notes the malice and anger behind his aunt's unhap-
piness over the breakdown of a world where she has occupied
a position of privilege:

> "I no longer pretend to understand the world". She is
> shaking her head yet still smilling her sweet menacing smile.
> "The world I knew has come crashing down around my
> ears. The things we hold dear are reviled and spat
> upon . . . . It's an interesting age you will live in—though
> I can't say I'm sorry to miss it. But it should be quite a
> sight, the going under of the evening land. That's us all
> right. And I'can tell you, my young friend, it is evening.
> It is very late".

Percy has captured the exact voice, the exact words, even
to the highfalutin reference to Oswald Splengler's *Decline of
the West* (*Abendland*, literally "evening land" in the original
German).

Critics have naturally theorized over the meaning of the
movies which are Binx's obsession. Everywhere he goes he is
reminded of movie personalities, movie plots. Some flashbacks
to movies are simply amusing. Other references seem pregnant
with symbolic meaning. Critics have suggested that the purpose
of the movies in *The Moviegoer* is to reflect the social reality

of Binx's world, or to mirror his fantasies, or (Coles's theory) to lay bare the condition of Binx's own soul. These interpretations are all true and indisputable. I would only add Percy's own interpretation, stated very directly: the movies for Binx are a way to orient himself amid the strangeness of life, to assure himself of ther eality of his existence in an inauthentic world. His term for this phenomenon is "certification".

This is what happens when Binx goes to see a film with his cousin Kate:

> *Panic in the Streets* with Richard Widmark is playing on Tchoupitoulas Street. The movie was filmed in New Orleans (the venue of *The Moviegoer*). Richard Widmark is a public health inspector who learns that a culture of cholera bacilla has gotten loose in the city. Kate watches, lips parted and dry. She understands my movie-going but in her own antic fashion. There is a scene which shows the very neighborhood of the theatre. Kate gives me a look—it is understood that we do not speak during the movie. Afterwards in the street, she looks around the neighborhood. "Yes it is certified now."
>
> She refers to a phenomenon of moviegoing which I have called certification. Nowadays when a person lives somewhere, in a neighborhood, the place is not certified for him. More than likely he will live there sadly and the emptiness which is inside him will expand until it evacuates the entire neighborhood. But if he sees a movie which shows his very neighborhood it becomes possible for him to live, for a time at least, as a person who is Somewhere and not Anywhere.

Perhaps the most touching incident in *The Moviegoer* has to do with a young man who is a tourist in New Orleans with his bride. They are uneasily walking down the touristy French Quarter, unhappy because they are surrounded by other tourists from other places exactly like themselves—all outsiders, all determined to capture the essence of this famous exotic city, all unable to do so. They catch sight of the movie actor William Holden. Holden asks a group of middle-aged tourists, "ladies from Harrisburg", for a match. They recognize

him, become confused. Holden then turns to the young man
for help. The young man rises to the occasion, whips out a
lighter, lights up for Holden, man to man. This encounter,
for Binx, the narrator, is the boy's salvation, his certification,
or authentication in existentialist language—at least for the
moment:

> The boy has done it. He has won the title to his own
> existence, as plenary an existence now as Holden's, by
> refusing to be stampeded like the ladies from Harrisburg.
> He is a citizen like Holden; two men of the world are they.

The tourist-outsider metaphor is one that Percy has developed in his essays at length, and it is closely connected with
that of the moviegoer. The tourist's distinguishing mark is
the camera. Why do people take photographs? Percy specula-
tes (in *Message in the Bottle*) that it is to reassure themselves
of their actual presence in the world, that they are not invisible
(like Ralph Ellison's black man in Harlem).

> A man is after all himself and no other, and not merely an
> example of a class of similar selves. If such a man is
> deprived of the means of being a self in a world made over
> by science for his use and enjoyment, he is like a ghost at a
> feast. He becomes invisible. That is why people in the
> modern age took photographs by the million; to prove
> despite their deepest suspicions to the contrary that they
> were not invisible.

Percy was a research scientist, but gave it up because he
felt that science, in its passion for classification, ignored the
human equation, the distinctions of personality, time, and
place—the existentialist "mystery":

> I called Harry's attention to the presence (of a sunbeam) but
> he shrugged and went on with his work. He was absolutely
> unaffected by the singularities of time and place. His abode
> was anywhere. It was all the same to him whether he catheri-
> zed a pig at four o'clock in the afternoon in New Orleans
> or at midnight in Transylvania. He was actually like one

of those scientists in the movies who don't care about anything but the problem in their heads—now here is a fellow who does have a "flair for research" and will be heard from. Yet I do not envy him. I would not change places with him if he discovered the cause and cure of cancer. For he is no more aware of the mystery which surrounds him than a fish is aware of the water it swims in.

Here then, we have a terribly serious and committed thinker who has turned novelist, and with considerable success. His limitations are not those of the propagandist, for Percy has the basic attributes of the natural story-teller: the ear, the eye, and the tongue. (Norman Mailer, of course, would insist that the novelist needs a good nose as well).

Language—the tongue—Percy treats with the utmost importance. He has studied the phenomenon of language and written about it with great acuteness and originality. For Percy language is the one indisputable human activity that plumbs the nature of man:

Language, which at first sight appears to be the most familiar *sort* of occurrence, an occurrence which takes place with other occurrences in the world—billiard balls hitting other billiard balls, barkings of dogs, crying of babies, sunrises, and rainfalls—is in reality utterly different from these events. The importance of a study of language, as opposed to a scientific study of a space-time event like a solar eclipse or rat behavior, is that as soon as one scratches the surface of the familiar and comes face to face with the nature of language, one also finds oneself face to face with the nature of man.

So the limitations of *The Moviegoer* do not spring from lack of seriousness or lack of talent. They spring instead paradoxically from too much seriousness, too much intelligence and talent brought to bear on one subject—however lightly the seriousness is borne, however adroitly the intelligence and talent are employed. This, of course, is the problem with all *romans a clef*; such novels, however deeply felt and thought, remain oddities—special pleadings for a cause or philosophy or movement, however world-shaking, and are thus ultimately oppressive. This is particularly true when the message is as pessimistic as Percy's, seeming to end in a cul-de-sac.

But not entirely. Percy is not the complete Cassandra. There is hope, since modern man still has the capacity for wonder, for a direct encounter with the mystery of reality. Binx goes on a hunting trip with friends who are desperately unhappy, desperately trying to assert their existence by carousing. He says:

> For some reason I sank into a deep melancholy. What good fellows they were, I thought, and how much they deserved to be happy. If only I could only make them happy . . . . "What's the matter with you, Binx?" they said at last. "My dear friends," I said to them. "I will say good-by and wish you well. I think I will go back to New Orleans and live in Gentilly". And there I have lived ever since, solitary and in wonder, wondering day and night, never a moment without wonder.

But the solitary state is only a way-station for the Christian existentialist seeking redemption. At the end of *The Moviegoer* Kate and Binx get married. They have become reconciled to, have acknowledged, their lost situation and will face it directly together. True, they will remain in the state of deep disquiet that is the hallmark of the age. But in marrying one another they have moved out of the most parlous situation of modern man—the one summed up in a quotation from Kierkegaard at the beginning of the book: "The specific character of despair is precisely this: it is unaware of being despair".

Percy offers some hope: he sees in the "postmodern consciousness . . . unlimited possibilities for both destruction and liberation, for an absolute loneliness or a rediscovery of community and reconciliation".

Community and reconciliation, the traditional Christian modes of authentic existence, are the existential gospel of Walker Percy, for which *The Moviegoer* is a brilliant metaphor.

11

"TOUTING THE VOID" :
A TREND IN FICTION AND CRITICISM

Kumkum Sangari

EXISTENTIALISM originated in the European experience of the twentieth century.   It has rapidly become a component of American fiction. Existentialism (my concern here is with the atheistic existentialism popularised by Heidegger and Sartre as opposed to the religious existentialism of Buber or Jaspers) as a literary phenomenon seems to have acquired universal overtones and become identified or even identical with "timeless" human experience. This seems ironic in the light of the fact that "the meaning of philosophical existentialism lay in regaining the full concretion of the historical subject."[1] In Europe existentialism took shape in response to the two world wars and the Cold War. In an important sense the emergence of existentialism coincided with the perception of the inability of the liberal belief in reason, progress, and the evolution of humanity, to cope with the feeling of futility and anarchy unleashed by the First World War. Though existential philosophers ranged in their political sympathies from Fascist (Heidegger) to Marxist (the later Sartre) or apolitical (Camus), broadly speaking their targets were the same: earlier rationalist philosophies with their abstract and essentialist categories, and all aspectso f contemporary culture (e.g. the complacencies of bourgeois values) which threatened or denied the individual's "authenticity". Existentialism proffered an ontology which centred on the existence of man and in this sense was a culmination of European individualism which had begun by abstracting the individual frcm scciety curing the Renaissance.

In much popular criticism of the American novel existentialism has been incorporated into a critical and creative value system which acts to transform it into an abstract, idealized, even transcendental philosophy. Such criticism subtracts from existentialism (what the later work of Sartre attempted to restore) its historical specificity as a philosophy which has both a local and causal origin, as well as a temporal significance.[2]

The purpose of this paper is not to make a case for a purist application of the philosophy, but to examine, from a rough sampling of literary criticism of Ernest Hemingway and Saul Bellow, how this transformation takes place, and which factors work to support it in the philosophy itself, in the American experience, and in the novels in question. It is necessary for critical practice to outline the affinities between contemporary American and European culture and to show how existentialism is adapted to the special needs and situation of the American novelist. The first section of this paper raises some questions about existentialism in Europe and America as well as about popularly known and applied existential concepts such as meaninglessness, alienation, and subjectivity. The second section examines critical commentary on Hemingway and Bellow in relation to their fiction and shows how existentialism becomes a new way of affirming traditional American values.

Since critical enquiry along existential lines, both in philosophy and in literary criticism, ranges over a span of centuries, it is important to locate those qualities within existentialism which are classed as "universal". John Macquarrie traces the origins of existentialism to a "pre-philosophy" mythological stage when the preoccupations with "the mystery of existence, infinitude and guilt, death and hope, freedom and meaning" already existed.[3] In a generalised sense he locates existential questions in the Hebrew religious prophets, in classic Greek culture, in Japanese Buddhist and Zen scholars, in the teaching of Christ, St. Paul, and St. Augustine, in Gnosticism, medieval German mysticism, and in Renaissance humanism. He concludes that the existential style of thought emerges in historical periods of insecurity, change, and turmoil. In tabulating the elements of pre-Kierkegaardian existentialism Mac-

quarrie overlooks the specific historical conjuctions in which
they appear and uses them in a more or less abstract sense in
an effort to construct a history of the philosophy. His
approach to existentialism as a philosophy is analogous to that
tendency in literary criticism which abstracts the so called
"modern" elements in literary works reflecting post-war and
post-industrial urban experiences (aimlessness, anonymity,
anxiety) and identifies them as both existential and universal.
The objection to this is immediately apparent—these elements
are historically specific and therefore neither timeless nor
universal.

The availability of existentialism to America lies partially
in the relation and the overlap between certain aspects of
existentialism and certain areas of modernism.[4] Existentialism
as a philosophy and modernism in the arts are responses forged in protest and despair to the same historical crisis. Existentialism has in common with modernism an anti-rational,
anti-bourgeois bias. Existentialism and modernism also share
a neglect of causality, a mutiple view of reality, a belief in the
ambiguity of existence, in personal sincerity and in personal
experience, as well as in subjectivity and interiority. Modernism has drawn freely on existential ideas of the contingency of
being to explain its own apprehension of disorder and upheaval.
Further, existentialism has provided a viable rationale to the
modern novel for experimenting with new techniques of
multiplicity, just as it now seems to be providing the postmodern novel with a rationale for its ahistorical, self-reflexive
fictions. This cross-fertilisation was inevitable given the eclectic and international tendency within modernism—modernism *is* partially an awareness of international trends. It is the
product of an age where by virtue of industrialisation Europe
and America had both reached a roughly similar stage of
development. It is not surprising therefore that modernism
and with it existentialism, should have been so rapidly accom-
modated within the American literary scene. To some extent
the American concern with the self as manifested by the
Transcendentalists (notably Whitman and Thoreau), the search
for an indigenous as well as an individual identity, and
William James's idea of the individual consciousness as an
"unfinished continuum" incapable of arriving at objectivity,[5]

provide a fertile soil for existentialist ideas. It is also possible to see how the practical failure of the social utopian ideals of the Twenties and Thirties led to a shift in the post-war novel from the societal to the psychical, as well as to see existentialism in America as opposing the bourgeois "cliches of affluence and conformity".[6] What often occurs in criticism on the American novel is a bunching together of the modern, the existential, and the American into an indiscriminate, and usually laudatory, whole, which then serves as an aid to the evaluation and analysis of fiction. This popular and generally accepted standpoint is abetted by certain factors within existentialism itself.

Ihab Hassan's discussion of the contemporary American novel in *Radical Innocence* is the literary counterpart of Macquarrie's *Existentialism* and worth detailing because of its representative nature. He equates the modern American experience, the conditions of which are gratuitous action, encounter with absurdity, anarchy, death, and nihlism, with the existential. The helpless individual is pitted against technology and all contemporary political systems. Victory is the process of defeat, the search is for self-definition and freedom, and the necessity is for retreat into selfhood. The "pattern of experience" in contemporary fiction is "largely existential" as it is composed of contradiction, chance, illusory choice, relativity of perception, chaos, absurdity, and nothingness. He dubs the existential form a "modern variant" of irony and proceeds to fuse his definition of the existential with Northrop Frye's definition of irony in the *Anatomy of Criticism*. Hassan concludes that existential awareness is based on the discovery of the "aboriginal Self" which in turn is the primal and anarchic American self. Existentialism for him is bound up with individual and society in dissolution; while alienation is "axiomatic" it is possible for the existential self to be affirmative and preserve a "radical kind of innocence". The existential hero, often an adolescent rebel-victim figure, is "transcendent by virtue of [his] nakedness rather than [his] communal authority".[7] In short, Hassan proffers an existential poetics of the novel which has as its basis a direct equation between the modern and the existential, and between the existential and the ironic mode. Therefore he is inclined to see irony as a timeless or ahistorical mode of perception: the implication that the existential is a "universal" view of man that is in some sense "given" is inescapable.

Hassan's account is representative of those tendencies in criticism which transform existentialism by grafting it to an insufficient liberal humanism. What results is a paradoxically affirmative value system capable of providing something like salvation for modern man. It will be useful to examine briefly such notions as meaninglessness, alienation, and subjectivity, which Hassan takes for granted and which usually support popular versions of existential philosophy.

The simplistic acceptance that life *is* absurd and meaningless, not that it *can* be seen as such, is as much an act of faith as the belief in God. John Clellon Holmes's 'Existentialism and the Novel' is illustrative. He ascribes an *a priori* existence to "the valueless abyss of modern life" which is then "discovered", so to speak, by Hemingway, Algren, and Kerouac.[8] While Holmes quite obscures the fact that the experience of valuelessness is itself subjective and societal. Alfred Kazin explains the predilection for meaninglessness more accurately as a "temporary fatigue" representing the "sometimes frolicsome despondency of intellectuals who see no great place for their moral influence—for changing things—in a future laid out in advance by technology."[9] The tendency to reify meaninglessness emerges from within existential thought itself. Theodor Adorno in his critique of Heidegger (in which he traces the tendency within Heidegger's extentialism to align itself with German nationalism) connects the experience of meaninglessness with the presence of leisure in a society which does not provide real freedom for the individual. Powerlessness and nothingness instead of being seen as a historical state of affairs are "eternalized" as the "pure essence" or substance of man: "actual, avoidable, or at least corrigible need" is revered as "the most humane element in the image of man."[10]

Alienation, which has a central place in existentialism, has acquired a broad significance and range of meaning in our century. In sociological terms alienation can mean loneliness, the absence of relationships, the feeling of disassociation from others or the explicit rejection of social values and norms, the sense of both powerlessness in the face of existing social structures as well as the sense of their meaninglessness.[11] While sociological categories of alienation register the inability to relate outside one's self, existential categories, on the other hand, indicate alienation *from the self* the failure to experience oneself which may come from an excess of conformity or a lack of individuality and spontaneity. Consequently they call into question the criteria of selfhood. Heidegger in *Being and Time* (1927) equates alienation with being cut off from one's potential "authentic" existence (a Being-toward-Death) by over-involvement in the present or a superficial understanding of oneself. For Sartre in *Being and Nothingness* (1943) alienation is the individual's experience of himself as an object, which is not a disparity to be overcome but a fact to be acknowledged. Alienation as a sociological category is a historical phenomenon susceptible to change, but as an existential category it is axiomatic becoming almost the quintessence of human nature. It is therefore both an eminently social *and* an asocial concept.

There is a tendency in criticism of the modern American novel to confuse or merge these two categories. Alienation is made an indestructible feature of human existence and sociological analysis is rendered irrelevant. The existential concept of alienation instead of being a separate and useful category simply helps to blur the socio-historical parameters of this predicament.[12] Such criticism ignores the historical relation and overlap of the sociological and the existential: the fact that the growth of the philosophy has paralleled, even responded to, the recognition of the isolation and ineffectuality of the individual in contemporary Western society, and has in turn given a dignity to his impotence.

The basis for the overvaluation of subjectivity lies in the importance existential thought gives to the conscious subject as meaning giver: the world acquires existence only to the extent that it enters individual experience. Truth and value are located in the self-discovery and the self-creation of the individual in his attempt to arrive at his authentic self and subsequently freedom. However, though such subjectivity is an invaluable dimension of the self, and Marcuse even gives it the status of "an antagonistic force in capitalistic society",[13] it cannot release the individual from facticity and factuality. The existential belief in subjectivity lends itself to simplistic notions such as that liberation must come from inside by changing man's conciousness or seeing the same reality differently. Karl Jaspers, for example, sees the obstacle to human freedom within man and not outside him in his social relationships. The hopeless circularity of this belief—given the historical determinants of the content of subjectivity itself— derives from the paradoxical nature of the individual's position within existential philosophy. On the one hand the isolated individual is seen as helpless in his struggle with a senseless world, on the other hand this very isolated consciousness is the source of his freedom: to define himself, to choose, to create new values. Subjectivity becomes a sovereign value. The existential point of view assists in setting up a special, insulating, and evasive relation to the sum total of reality even while setting itself up as the sum total of reality. Subjectivity can become an escape from social wholes, from the network of relationships in which the individual is embedded. The valorization of subjectivity is often accompained by a fascination with the here-and-now and so runs the danger of reducing existence to the present instant. The later Sartre recognized that seeing the transient as an absolute can become a mode of evading the "future".[14] The centrality of the subjective self in existential thought lends itself both to an easy nonconformism and to an upholding of individual liberty against everything that appears to threaten it. It allows a dismissal of ideas, systematisations, and disciplined modes of behaviour, a rejection of external determinants as reducing moral responsibility and human freedom, a denial of any link between choice and the circumstances in which it takes place. It can lead further to an aggrandizement of failure, violence, and death as in the work of Jaspers, Sartre and Heidegger respectively. Finally such aggrandizement allows the "authentication" of failure, violence, and death.

Extistentialism becomes a means for transcending the limiting social environment. By making subjectivity a supreme value some critical commentary on Hemingway and Bellow elevates their protagonists into symbols of the general human condition, of a transcendental conception of humanity. Subjectivity becomes the central component of a humanism in which an exaltation of the nature of "Man", measure of all things, is conjoined with his refusal to be defined either by his environment or by history. The premium placed on the subjective individual self increases in proportion to his actual dehumanization in society. The intactness of the self then must be maintained at any cost. Existentialism in some popular readings of the modern American novel is transformed into a liberal humanist value. Liberal humanism put its belief in a universal human nature, insisted on the freedom of the individual to realize his human capacity, and opposed those social institutions which denied the individual his right to self development. When grafted on existentialism (or vice versa) it allows the individual to be exalted even while he is shown as helpless. This in turn becomes a means of reconciling the individual to his historical plight.

Jerry H. Bryant's *The Open Decision* exemplifies these tendencies.[15] He sees existential thinking as *the* intellectual background to the postwar American novel, and the postwar American novel as virtually a paean of what he considers to be affirmative human values i.e. subjectivity, relativity. Existential philosophy (his version is compounded of Husserl, Heidegger, Sartre, and Camus) becomes a moral system which is "good" because it is "real", and because it affirms human glory in the absence of God. In this kind of critical practice existentialism acquires a double value: that of rebellion through its exaltation of rebel (who is opposed to the "abslutist" revolutionary with fixed ideas) and outlaw figures, and that of conformity to values derived from liberal humanism. Thus the existential hero and the literary critic can serve to maintain existing values even while appearing not to do so. It is a matter of some historical interest to see how existentialism which emerged in response to the problematic relation between individual behaviour, social function, and public morality, should itself be esconced as a sovereign morality with as much force in literary criticism as the "felt life" of Henry James or that of the "lived" of F. R. Leavis once had.

Another significant transmutation which becomes apparent from Bryant's book is that of the self made man—epitome of the American Dream—into the existential self created man.

This self referential hero of the modern and postmodern American novel is descended from the individualism within the American Dream: the American Dream and the success ethic brought up to date as it were. This transmutation extends to negative states of being—despair, alienation, and meaningless-ness—which are now regarded as broadly human affirmations. The existential vocabulary provides the critic with an easy evaluation of experience, and transforms a liberal humanism, which has forfeited the progressive role it had in the nineteeth century, into a positive, contemporary, and usable category. The ironic result of this revitalization is that existentialism itself falls prey to the very essentialism it questioned so radically in its European heydey.

The tendency, stemming from existentialism, which sees retreat into selfhood as a means of salvation, provides a foundation for a religious optimism about the fate of the universe. This in turn leads to the search for redemption in every modern novel. For example Ihab Hassan's new hero, the "rebel-victim", bearer of an "existential" and "self-made" morality which is full of "ironies and ambiguities" is endowed nevertheless with a "will" which is "always in some sense redemptive."[16] Some of the basis for seeing existentialism as salvation has come from extra literary sources. Ernst Brei-sach's *Introduction to Modern Existentialism* is paradigmatic in this respect. He seems to be constructing a streamlined and up-to-date philosophy *from* existentialism. He makes the following propositions: existentialism is a new humanism opposed to totalitarian systems since it upholds tolerance; there is a kinship between true Western democratic ideals and existentialism, the "most important contribution of existentia-lism to the democratic form of life . . . lies in the rebirth of a true and genuine individualism" which is opposed to theories of the conditioned man. Existentialism provides a new con-cept of liberty to refurbish the old American one, a liberty which "resides as a potential force only in the individual and can not be produced by laws, institutions, or a natural bene-volent force."Finally existentialism is seen as hailing a religious renaissance which is not just a "salvage operation" "to rescue a supposedly declining western culture" : "it desires to speak of and to man and not merely of and to contemporary Western man". Breisach underrates the existential critique of contemporary Western life and thought. For him its pertinence derives from "the insistence on always discovering the general human predicament beneath the covers of temporary crises."[17]

The transformation of existentialism into a transcendental humanism and a religion of universal relevance is complete—the mystique of existentialism comes into being aided and abetted by the potential solipsism of the philosophy itself. Marcuse has pointed out that "the existential as such is exempt from any rational standard or norm lying beyond it; it is itself the absolute norm and is inaccessible to any and all rational criticism and justification."[18] The criticism discussed here mirrors this antirational position by taking for granted both the absolute authority of the existential stance and its task of transformation and application.

Hemingway and Bellow, commonly upheld as existential novelists, have close links with the European sensibility—Hemingway by virtue of his expatriation and Bellow by virtue of his self conscious intellectualism. Bellow makes a more self conscious use of existential ideas and vocabulary than Hemingway. Much critical commentary on Hemingway presupposes an existential terminology. Hugh Kenner sees Hemingway's role as first "recorder" and then "experiencer of authenticities".[19] For Alan Kennedy the way to authenticity is through action: action necessitates a confrontation with death, increases the sense of being oneself through forcing recognition of the not-self and is possible only when the reality of the external world is unquestioned.[20] Similarly, the pattern of Hemingway's fiction for Wiley Lee Umphlett is that of a recurring encounter in which he creates a sense of victory out of defeat—the heroes begin to face life when they face death. As in *The Old Man and the Sea* Hemingway, "in placing emphasis on the quality of an action expended to achieve a goal rather than on the act of achieving the goal itself, expresses the measure of the man through his performance and not necessarily through his accomplishment." Santiago's isolation and encounter with the marlin lend definition, meaning, and value to "an existence that would otherwise seem abortive".[21] Leslie Fiedler, in consonance with Daniel J. Schneider, declares that Hemingway loved nothingness, death, and failure more than being, life, and success; his "authentic work has a single subject : the flirtation with death, the approach to the void", his later work in which he "betrayed death and the void" is the counterfeit of his best.[22] Hemingway is an existential novelist for John Clellon Holmes and his power lies in his "instinctual acknowledgement of the tragedy of meaninglessness" and the necessity to overcome despair.[23] For Robert Penn Warren, John Griffith, Michael Friedburg, and E. M. Halliday the Hemingway protagonist is in his search for meaning thrown back on his own private discipline: his ethic of behaviour, his existential focus on "conduct", his preoccupation with "expertise" have great subjective value and attempt to develop a way of facing death.[24] Harry Levin in an eassy on Hemingway's style speaks of his "exaltation of the instant", his trust in experience and his effort to restore the correspondence between words and things.[25] Halliday's essay relates style to content: for both Hemingway and his heroes the inevitability of death "merely emphasizes the need to live each moment properly and skillfully, to sense judiciously the texture of every fleeting act and perception."[26] Alfred Kazin reiterates this and adds that Hemingway, deeply concerned with the preservation of the "intactness" of the self, identified "literature with the *act* of writing, writing as the word-for-word struggle against the murkiness of death".[27] Nemi D' Agostino holds that within the violence of his time Hemingway emerged as "the upholder of the only humanism which seemed possible at the time". Aware of the "collapse of a moral order", full of an "extreme disillusion and distrust of all values" he takes to "the exaltation of daring, of the beauty of violence and the beauty of death" ; in his later work, however, he turns this code into "a preposterous and unironical search for excitement for its own sake" and so cuts himself off from historical development and takes "refuge in irresponsible and self-complacent isolation". Life for Hemingway remains a "solitary struggle, a desperate fever of action, conscious of having no sense or reason beyond itself. Nothing can be justified, bettered or saved, no problem that can really be set or solved".[28]

The picture that emerges of Hemingway is that of an artist who has, through an obsession with authenticity and death, forged an ethic of action and conduct and a means of utilizing the present moment in the face of a confrontation with defeat and nada. Yet despite the odds Hemingway is seen as succeeding in the assertion of value and as the upholder of the only kind of humanism now possible. Given the ease with which Hemingway's work fits into the existential framework, it is not surprising that his fiction is in turn judged by its failure or success in living up to "normative" existential ideas. It is in consonance with this ascribed humanism and its essentialist constituents that his work should even be interpreted as religious allegory—Joseph Waldmeir demonstrates that *The Old Man and the Sea* is built upon "the great abstractions—love and truth and honour and loyalty and pride and humility".[29]

The smoothness with which Hemingway's life and work slide into existential categories obscures his real relation to the philosophy which is far from straightforward. Hemingway's style, generally regarded as supremely expressive of his philosophy of life, is illustrative. The simple style with its emphasis on concretion, the exaltation of the instant, the casual accuracy and the heavy load of implication, the unreflective integrity and the celebrated restoration of the purity of word and meaning are seen and described as the reconstitution of sincerity. However, the insistence on the empirical does more than this. The famous first chapter of *A Farewell to Arms* (1929) combines vagueness with specificity in a masterly way: the war is located in an indefinite time sequence consisting of "that year", "the next year" and "last year" even as the narrative establishes the facticity of the mountains, river, boulders, pebbles, soldiers, within the seasonal chronology of summer, fall, rain, and snow.[30] The purity of a style which has been constituted to express and overcome the incongruity between rhetoric and experience, word and meaning, self and world, functions to delink the individual and his experience from the social, political, and economic framework. The centrality of the immediate experience and the establishment of the here-and-now as the hub of reality can become a technique for the evasion of a more composite reality. Frederic Henry is a man minus all the surplus of civilization: religion, politics, history, culture,

family, ideas. But the nonconformity is more apparent than
real. By apparently reducing him to the constituents of his
subjectivity and empirical existence Hemingway succeeds not
so much in re-establishing contact with existence as such as in
creating a mythology of Being which once again goes beyond
the factuality and facticity of existence. In fact Hemingway
supplies a pattern for being human, more specifically being a
man, which though it appears as intrinsic and asocial is derived
from a social and American value structure and constitutes
an "existentialization" of accepted values. To put it another
way, Hemingway integrates the existential with an inescapably
essentialist value structure rooted in the contemporary social
fabric.

It would be helpful to examine these two elements in
Hemingway's work—the existential and its opposite, the
essential. Hemingway's existential value structure depends
heavily on subjective versions of authenticity and death similar
to those developed by Heidegger. For Heidegger in *Being
and Time* (1927) inauthentic existence is living in fear of "theyness". True *Dasein* or being is self possession, the repudiation
of "theyness". Falling into inauthenticity is a necessary component of everyday existence and is in fact "the inevitable
quality which characterizes an individual's involvement with
others and with the phenomenal world".[31] The individual's
struggle is for repossession of the self. The problem with this
notion of authenticity is that the sense of belonging to oneself is formal and not related to the social and psychological
obstacles of being oneself. The sovereign mark of authenticity
is the person at his own disposal, his own possession, with no
regard of the fact that the individual is caught up in a "determining objectivity". The conception of selfness, as Adorno
points out, is abstract even as it gives being and meaning since
it has "no substratum but its own concept." So unlimited
self possession becomes equal to freedom, subjectivity becomes the arbitrary "judge of authenticity". Finally, authenticity becomes "objectively discoverable" in the subject as
observed by the observing subject: it becomes a reified attribute, an "object", a "manner of behaviour" which can be
"prefixed", a "mythically imposed fate".[32]

Hemingway tries to actualize the heroic ideal of authenticity

outside the objective social context. Even while he searches
for further areas of action he instates himself as the supreme
judge of authenticity. *Death in the Afternoon* (1932) presents
bullfighting as aesthetic spectacle and proof of the bullfighter's
sincerity which is a combination of his style and concentration.
The fight is to be tragedy for the bull. The fighter must
increase the danger to him at will yet remain "within the
rules provided for his protection".[33] The bullfighter glories
in an art which will die with him: the zest of his occupation
comes as much from being the target as from being the potential killer. The special mark of sincerity which distinguishes
him from other men is the detachment which comes from
facing death every day—the constantly renewed act of self
possession in the offering up of oneself for destruction. However close it might seem superficially this is not the authenticity Heidegger envisaged because it does not entail the forging
of new values. The bullfighter's supreme act of self possession
does not help him to reclaim his independence and purity
from the "they", but lays him open at the moment of his
greatest potential grandeur to judgement by values of the world
which can easily be classed as inauthentic. The bullfighter
must possess courage, honest ability, wrist magic, and aesthetic
vision. In the killing of bulls he must display honour, dignity,
passion, and style. The apparent stripping down to an
authentic selfness is a reassertion of old values under a new
guise. The structure of the existential encounter is used to
incorporate, elevate, and authenticate the machismo element
which already exists within the American value system. The
raw violence of killing the bull is assimilated into the notion
of style. *Death in the Afternoon* uses an objective documen-
tary framework consisting of eyewitness and camera records of
the bullfights, an accurate account of the techniques used and
a glossary of terms. However, the underlying structure is the
persuasive one of initiation. Authenticity is not only a reified
and discoverable quality but one which can be introduced,
defined, and perhaps even learned.

The tendency to incorporate established and therefore
essentialist values into an existential framework is more pronounced in *The Old Man and the Sea* (1952). Santiago is shown
as having complete disposal over himself and at the same time

as the archetype of simplicity, courage, and endurance. The machismo element in him is apparent from his hero worship of Joe Di Maggio and his twenty hour struggle with a black athlete. Santiago's existential discovery of himself appears in a different light when he is recognized as sharing the characteristics of the American folk-cum-frontier-cum-athletic hero: "self-reliance, perserverance, self-assertiveness, competitiveness, practicality, idealism, and an extraordinary physical prowess".[34] Santiago's defeat is seen as a victory, not because the American success ethic has lost its potency for Hemingway but because the existential ethic centred around authenticity and the value of the moment allows him to invert it into creditable forms of failure. Santiago's taciturnity then is a deceptive mask for the old American values—the existential exposure of the self is hedged in by recognizable norms.

The situation of the typical Hemingway hero is paradoxical. He proves his authentic existence in a way which belies his separateness from contemporary society. At the same time he is insulated from reality, his context is "beyond and apart from what moves the world".[35] The extent of this paradox becomes apparent on examining Hemingway's obsession with death. The primacy that Hemingway gives to death is akin to Heidegger's ethic and shares some of its myopia. For Sartre death is the culminating absurdity but Heidegger finds a way from the anticipation of death to authentic existence and freedom. In *Being and Time* Heidegger sees authentic being as a *being-toward-death*. Since death is the highest possibility of existence, it "permits us to view *Dasein* in its totality". Death endows a unity to existence by setting a limit to it. The "moment before death" is "decisive" for in it "the past, present, and future are gathered into the unity of the resolute self," which becomes "aware of its finitude and nothingness through the ontological experience of anxiety in the face of death",—this is "the way that leads to the encounter with being".[36] Only in the foreknowledge of death are both the senselessness and significance of human existence revealed.

George Steiner applauds Heidegger's *being-toward-death* since it is "inalienable": death, "the one existential potentiality which no enslavement, no promise, no power of 'theyness' can take away from individual man, is the fundamental truth of the meaning of being... The possibility of *Dasein* depends on, makes sense only in respect of...death. The one cannot *be* without the other. ... Authentic death has to be striven for... The taking upon oneself through *Angst*, of this existential 'terminality' is the absolute condition of human freedom.... FREEDOM TOWARDS DEATH."[37] Adorno taking the opposite view, (a view of equal relevance to Hemingway) criticizes Heidegger for making death, which negates and destroys *Dasein*, "the core of the self" and "the essential character of subjectivity itself". Death assumes godlike proportions and becomes "an absolute in the form of an icon". Mortality becomes primary, the world secondary. Authenticity finds its "norm and ideal" in death. Death is seen as "the ontological foundation of totality" and the "meaning giving element in the midst of... fragmentation". Isolation and "non-relatedness" which are a part of death form the substratum of selfness —an attitude of total self-sufficiency. The anticipation of death becomes "a mode of behaviour" which is "expected to acquire dignity by accepting such a necessity speechlessly and without reflection." The "dissolution of the self" becomes an "inflexibly stoic positing of the self" and so makes of self a "negative principle". Thus extremes of pain authenticate the subject. The dangers of making death "qualitatively superior" to other phenomena are the danger of sublimating it, stylizing it, and "falsely" cleansing it of "misery and stench".[38]

For Hemingway death becomes the high point of individualism. His protagonists are put in extreme or limit situations, their authenticity is measured by the way they face death (or as in *Death in the Afternoon* the way they inflict death). The preoccupation with death insulates his protagonists from the world and constitutes their self-sufficiency. Santiago's self-sufficiency comes from the anticipation and unreflecting acceptance of his death. Hemingway effects a simultaneous desacralisation and sacralization of death by making it both ordinary and extraordinary at the same time. In his effort to present death as the simplest and most fundamental truth ("one of the simplest things of all and the most fundamental is violent death")[39] Hemingway mystifies it. There is a visible struggle in *A Farewell to Arms* to abstract death, and by that token life, of all meaning. When Frederic Henry is wounded he feels himself "rush bodily out of myself and out and out and out and all the time bodily in the wind."[40] By concentrating on its purely physical nature death is shorn of religious, philosophical, and political associations. The way the individual faces death is the supreme test: Catherine faces it by making it her very own—she strives to die well. Hemingway is replacing one brand of heroism with another. Since death is at once a wiping out and an assertion of value Hemingway manages to make it the culminating value in a series of values which range from courage and stoicism to machismo. On the surface he privatizes death in an existential manner, beneath he creates a heroic ideal out of the existing value structure. Death in his fiction appears to be a self-contained whole—the inalienable possibility Heidegger speaks of—but upon examination it leads straight back to American frontier values like assertiveness and physical strength. In 'The Snows of Kilimanjaro' (1936) a dying writer who has failed in his writing makes a conscious effort to regain his authenticity in the face of death. Having succumbed to "theyness" by becoming a possession of his "rich bitch" wife, seeing his selfhood as a finite quantity which he has squandered, he makes a last effort in the moments before death. The effort consists of a true recognition of the present face of death and a recollection of his past life. He remembers moments of sensuous and palpable living as well as instances of manly assertion—war, displays of strength, whoring, affairs with women, trout fishing—which may never now be written about. Death becomes the structural culmination of this kind of experience. Instead of freeing the dying writer from "theyness" it becomes the final moment within a cult of action that is typical of Hemingway: "The one experience that he had never had he was not going to spoil now."[41] Death appears to be a secular icon for Hemingway. In *Death in the Afternoon* "the final sword thrust" is "the moment of truth".[42] However, this moment of truth, as the photographs of dead and dying bulls and bullfighters show, is hygienically cleansed of its actual misery, pain, and violence. All these are assimilated into a stylized and spurious version of an existential reality. Death *is* the meaning giver for Heidegger. In Hemingway's fiction death masquerades as the meaning giver—in fact it is the ultimate sensation— and in facing it in areas of increasing danger Hemingway is merely rescuing it from boredom.

Critical commentary on Bellow which acclaims him as an existential novelist usually claims for him a redemptive and transcendental humanism. Howard Harper and R.R. Dutton define Bellow's existentialism in Sartrean terms: man himself is the measure of all things and he is what he chooses to be. They see Bellow's heroes as drifting aimlessly, indulging in gratuitous action, haunted by or confronting death, trapped and alienated yet searching for identity and meaning.[43] Dutton stresses the value of subjectivity for Bellow, and like Nathan A. Scott Jr. rejects all social determinism for Bellow's characters. For Scott the "central moments" in the experience of a Bellow character are those in which he, "transcending the immediate pressures of his environment and the limiting conditions of the social matrix, asks himself some fundamental questions about the nature of his own humanity."[44] Dutton locates Bellow in the humanist tradition for continuing to exalt the nature of man. For Harper Bellow's protagonists are initiated into "a larger transcendental conception of humanity" which transcends the limited and limiting dimension of "pure reason".[45] For Scott though Bellow's protagonists are burdened by "the pressure of concrete circumstance" and the "bitter taste" of "inauthenticity" the novels still move towards "disburdenment" and reconciliation. He sees Bellow as being critical of such existential notions as alienation, *Angst*, and nothingness. He ascribes this partially to Bellow's deepening "conviction that the way into blessedness and felicity is the way of what Martin Heidegger called *Gelassenheit* of acquiescent submission to the multileveled and radical mystery of existence, the way of *falling*-into-Peace." But *Gelassenheit* need not "entail any abdication from the social contract" for Bellow "knows that the world supports and confirms the sacrament of selfhood only in the degree to which it is organized along the lines of some viable form of coexistence."[46]

Nathan Scott does not entirely reject the determination of the individual by external factors—he attempts to have it both ways by combining the sacramental view of self with a recognition of concrete factuality and fellowmanhood. Similarly, John. J. Clayton takes an ambiguous stand. Bellow for him has an existential sensibility which takes cognizance of the despair, alienation, and emptiness of modern life, yet takes a stand against the "Wasteland" and opts for "brotherhood and community". Bellow values individuality but sees social redemption as coming through replacing individuality by concern for others. Clayton takes a moralistic stance and opts for a non-solipsistic existentialism. His rejection of the negative character of existentialism comes from the affirmative character of his liberal humanist standpoint. So we are given a portrait of Bellow as a critic of existentialism who had nevertheless accepted its central assumptions; living in the here-and-now, rejecting the "constructed" self, obsessed with pure being, accepting the "necessity of confronting one's own death in order to become authentic",[47] Max F. Schulz depicts Bellow as a moderate existentialist who rejects reason and modern positivism in favour of a more encompassing embrace of experience—of the whole man. Bellow resists both existential despair and nada as well as naive optimism and settles for a humanism which accepts the pain of existence. The contours of this humanism are now familiar: the heart as a guide to morality, the psychic and spiritual triumph over a death bravely confronted, the celebration of individual identity while aiming for an equilibrium between the individual and society, the maintenance of the "integral self"—"civilization exists, Bellow would have it, only so long as the individual can retain his selfness intact."[48] All these critical commentaries find some kind of redemption in Bellow's fiction whether it is affirmation of man's unique individuality, the celebration of the whole man, the acceptance of community, submission to the mystery of existence, or as in Schulz, the reification of subjectivity. For Schulz subjectivity is the chief constituent of humanism—a triumphant interiority rescues man and the world from destruction.

Bellow's relation to both existentialism and humanism is oblique; the so called redemptive aspects of his fiction in fact result in a strange quiescence which reveals the true nature of his concern for man. Existential notions provide a value structure for the middleclass urban neuroses and the domesticated sexual dilemmas of Bellow's protagonists. Josephine Hendin has called the intelligence of Bellow's heroes "a diversion from the real world"—"ideas provide relief" from personal problems but "no solutions".[49] In *Herzog* (1964) the eponymous hero plays with ideas and has at the same time a scorn for fixed conceptual categories ranging from existentialism to historical materialism. A wide range of modern European thought is compressed into his consciousness and becomes the constituent of his subjectivity. His intellectual sophistication conceals his actual distance from his social context, the narrow and domestic confines of his experience. Despite his contempt for "Alienation" and "touting the Void" Herzog's own consciousness is a good example of the existential concern with selfness. His consciousness has an essential circularity: it traps all ideas including meaninglessness, helplessly shuffles them around, and makes an abortive effort to find redemptive elements within its own constitution. The individual consciousness seems to be Bellow's version of fate—the significant theme in *Herzog* for him is "the imprisonment of the individual in a shameful and impotent privacy" which is not an "intellectual privilege" but "another form of bondage".[50] Despite this recognition on Bellow's part the failure of his protagonists to break out becomes by an existential inversion of the success ethic his badge of success. By presenting all ideas as equally the content of individual consciousness all ideas are given equal weight. Herzog becomes a consumer of philosophies.

Bellow's fiction works towards a liberal eclecticism and an intellectual pluralism which are, in the final analysis, modes of social accommodation and compliance. The upholding of wholeness as a value works towards the same end. The fractured, paranoic, atomized consciousness of his heroes constantly implies the desirable opposite of wholeness. But the questions of whether "reality deserves being at one with", whether reality itself does not "deny" men wholeness and whether this reality itself needs changing are never quite formulated.[51] It is not surprising that at the end of the novel Herzog should sink into a prone passivity and find a quasi-mystical peace. *Herzog* and *Mr. Sammler's Planet* (1970) present a view of man which elevates his selfness at the same time as it acknowledges his social impotence and futility. This combination works as an assertion of faith in "Man" as well as a

simultaneous rationalization of his helplessness. Bellow's
fiction, or at least the novels in question, imply an unchange-
able social reality in which the individual's impotence becomes
a universal category and must therefore, along with his
subjectivity, be elevated if some semblance of humanism is to
remain intact. So Dutton's description of Herzog—as the
intellectual suffering from self-doubt regarding his social
relevance as well as a symbol of the general human condition—
unwittingly reveals the paradox on which Bellow's fiction
seems to be based.

Bellow's questioning of existential notions and his use of
the existential perspective as an overlay of doubt on the affirmations of the humanist tradition must be read in this context.
In *Mr Sammler's Planet* Sammler lives in full consciousness of
contingency, age, and death. Death is the only certainty
and all his experience seems to have led him towards it:
being forced to dig his own grave then being buried in it,
the ecstatic killing of the soldier, the seeking out of death
in going to the battlefront in Israel and then to Elya Gruner's
deathbed. However, both Bellow and Sammler are semi-
humorous about these very preoccupations. Given the paradoxical nature of his fiction Bellow can afford to be humorous
about the preoccupations of his protagonists even as he presents their experience in all its existential intensity. The
suspicion that this humour evades responsibility grows if the
ludic structure of his fiction is examined. *Herzog* is a play
of consciousness with itself, with others (for example Herzog's
incessant letter writing), and as a fictional construct. The
ludic element lies in the temporary and illusory assumption
of individual freedom, mastery, and self transcendence. The
fiction constructs of Bellow are partly critical of status quo
i.e. satirizing, stripping, or reassembling contemporay modes
of perception, and partly disguised affirmations of contemporary American values. The ludic structure can "contain"
existential notions, while through an intelligent use of these
notions Bellow can make tolerable the pluralism of contemporary American culture. Existentialism functions as both
weapon of criticism and a mode of compliance—a disguise
for an indigenous value system based on a liberal humanism.

For both Hemingway and Bellow the existential perspective

functions as a gesture towards the autonomy of the individual but in the fiction of both the content of this autonomy is in doubt. There is a tangential though significant relationship between Hemingway's and Bellow's use of existentialism and contemporary American values. However, for some critics of the American novel existential notions provide a handy means for maintaining their own value systems. If any effort is to be made to see existentialism in perspective —both as a critical response to the contemporary situation as well as a philosophy which contains the potential for being transformed into an instrument for buttressing that very situation—then this is more than a significant trend. The tendency in postwar Europe has been for existential philosophy to align itself overtly with politics, as in Sartre's Marxism, or to become apolitical as with Camus. In America there is a discernible tendency to revitalize an existing liberal humanism with existential ideas and so inject the existential stance with an ethical and religious tincture.

NOTES

1. Herbert Marcuse, *Negations* (Harmondsworth, Middlesex: Penguin Books, 1972), p. 32.
2. *Search for a Method* (1963). Reprinted as 'Marxism and Existentialism' in *Existentialism Versus Marxism: Conflicting Views on Humanism*, ed. George Novack (New York: Dell, 1966), pp. 175-205.
3. *Existentialism* (New York, 1972; rept. Harmondsworth, Middlesex: Penguin Books, 1973) p. 21.
4. The characteristics of modernism have been succintly defined by Malcolm Bradbury and James McFarlane in *Modernism: 1890-1930*, ed. M. Bradbury and J.McFarlane (Harmondsworth, Middlesex: Penguin Books, 1976) pp. 19-56, and Irving Howe in *Decline of the New* (London: Victor Gollancz, 1976), pp. 3-33.
5. See William J. Gavin, "William James and the Importance of 'The Vague'," *Cultural Hermeneutics*, 3, No. 3 (1976), pp. 245-65.
6. See Jonathan Baumbach, *The Landscape of Nightmare : Studies in the Contemporary American Novel* (1965; rpt. New York: New York University Press, 1967) and Ihab Hasasn, *Contemporary American Literature : 1945-72* (New York : Frederick Ungar, 1973), p. 8.
7. *Radical Innocence : Studies in the Contemporary American Novel* (Princeton, N.J.: Princeton University Press, 1961), pp. 19-20, 114, 115, 120, 325.

8. *Chicago Review*, 13, No. 2 (1959), 141-51.

9. *Bright Book of Life; American Novelists and Storytellers from Hemingway to Mailer* (Toronto, 1971; rpt. Boston: Little, Brown and Co., 1973), p. 245.

10. *The Jargon of Authenticity*, trans. Knut Tarnowski and Fredrick Will (1964; rpt. London: Routledge and Kegan Paul, 1973), pp. 34-36, 65.

11. For a detailed discussion see Richard Schacht, *Alienation* (London: George Allen and Unwin, 1971).

12. The result of this can be seen in the social application of existentialism. Gerald Graff has shown in 'Babbitt at the Abyss: the Social Context of Postmodern American fiction' (*Triquarterly*, pp. 31-34 (1975), pp. 305-37) that since the sixties in America alienation has ceased to be a predicament and become a "historically conscious *style*", which is stimultaneously trivialised and fashionable.

13. *The Aesthetic Dimension : Toward a Critique of Marxist Aesthetics*, trans. Herbert Marcuse and Erica Sherover (Boston: 1978; rpt. London: Macmillan, 1979), p. 38.

14. 'Marxism and Existentialism', *Existentialism versus Marxism*, p. 186.

15. *The Open Decision : The Contemporary American Novel and Its Intellectual Background* (New York: The Free Press, 1970).

16. *Contemporary American Literature*, p. 25.

17. (New York: Grove Press, 1962), pp. 228-36.

18. *Negations*, p. 35.

19. *A Homemade Self : The American Modernist Writers* (New York: Alfred A. Knopf, 1975), p. 145.

20. *The Protean Self : Dramatic Action in Contemporary Fiction* (London: Macmillan, 1974), pp. 55-56.

21. *The Sporting Myth and the American Experience : Studies in Contemporary American Fiction* (Lewisburg: Bucknell University Press, 1975), pp. 77, 86.

22. *'Waiting for the End'* (New York: Stein and Day, 1970), pp. 15-16; Daniel J. Schneider, "Hemingway's *A Farewell to Arms :* The Novel as pure Poetry", in *Ernest Hemingway: Five Decades of Criticism*, ed. Linda Wagner (East Lansing, Michigan: State University Press, 1974).

23. Holmes, p. 146.

24. Robert Penn Warren, Ernest Hemingway", in *Ernest Hemingway: Five Decades*; John Griffith, "Rectitude in Hemingway's Fiction: How Rite makes Right", in *Hemingway in Our Time*, eds. Richard Astro and Jackson J. Benson (Corvallis : Oregon State University Press, 1974); Michael Friedburg, "Hemingway and the Modern Metaphysical Tradition", in *Hemingway in Our Time*; E.M. Halliday "Hemingway's Ambiguity: Symbolism and Irony", in *Hemingway: A Collection of Critical Essays*, ed. Robert P. Weeks (Englewood Cliffs, N.J.: Prentice Hall, 1962).

25. Harry Levin, "Observations on the Style of Ernest Hemingway", in *Hemingway : A Collection of Critical Essays*.

26. Halliday, *Hemingway : A Collection of Critical Essays*, p. 53.

27. *Bright Book of Life*, pp. 5, 16.

28. Nemi D' Agostino, "The Later Hemingway", in *Hemingway : A Collection of Critical Essays*, pp. 152, 153, 158, 159.

29. "Confiteor Hominem: Ernest Hemingway's Religion of Man", in *Hemingway : A Collection of Critical Essays*, p. 161.

30. (Harmondsworth, Middlesex: Penguin Books, 1966), pp. 7-8.

31. George Steiner, *Heidegger* (Hassocks, Sussex: Harvester Press, 1978), p. 95.

32. *The Jargon of Authenticity*, pp. 114-27.

33. *Death in the Afternoon* (Harmondsworth, Middlesex : Penguin Books, 1973), p. 23.

34. Listed by Wiley Lee Umphlett in *The Sporting Myth*, p. 32.

35. Ernest Fischer, *The Necessity of Art*, trans. Anna Bostock (1959; rpt. Harmondsworth, Middlesex: Penguin Books, 1964), p. 100.

36. Macquarrie, *Existentialism*, pp. 152, 153, 171, 196.

37. *Heidegger*, pp. 101-02.

38. *The Jargon of Authenticity*, pp. 137-169.

39. *Death in the Afternoon*, p. 6.

40. *A Farewell to Arms*, p. 46.

41. *The Snows of Kilimanjaro and Other Stories* (Harmondsworth, Middlesex : Penguin Books, 1975), p. 23.

42. *Death in the Afternoon*, p. 165.

43. *Desperate Faith : A Study of Bellow, Salinger, Mailer, Baldwin and Updike* (Chapel Hill: University of North Carolina Press, 1967); *Saul Bellow* (Boston: Twayne Publishers, 1971).

44. *Three American Novelists : Mailer, Bellow, Trilling* (Notre Dame, Indiana : University of Notre Dame Press, 1973), p. 105.

45. *Desperate Faith*, p. 20.

46. *Three American Novelists*, p. 108, 113, 134, 224.

47. *Saul Bellow: In Defense of Man* (1968; rpt. Bloomington: Indiana University Press, 1979), pp. 4, 120.

48. *Radical Sophistication: Studies in Contemporary Jewish/American Novelists* (Athens, Ohio : Ohio University Press, 1969), pp. 128-29.

49. *Vulnerable People : A View of American Fiction since 1945* (Oxford: Oxford University Press, 1978), p. 213.

50. Quoted by Tony Tanner, *City of Words : American Fiction: 1950-1970* (New York : Harper and Row, 1971), p. 304.

51. *The Jargon of Authenticity*, p. 142.

THE JAIN BIRD-HOSPITAL IN DELHI

William Meredith

Outside the hotel window unenlightened pigeons
weave and dive like Stukas on their prey,
apparently some tiny insect brother.
(In India, the attainment of non-violence
is considered a proper goal for men and women).
If one of the pigeons should fly into the illusion

of my window and survive (life is no illusion
to the wounded) he could be taken across town to the bird-
hospital, where Jains, skilled medical men,
repair the feathery sick and broken victims.
There, in reproof of violence
and of nothing else, live Mahavira's brothers and sisters.

To this small, ancient order of monks and nuns
it is bright Vishnu and dark Shiva who constitute illusion.
They trust in faith, cognition and non-violence
to release them from the cycle of rebirth. They think that birds
and animals—like us, some predators, some prey—
should be ministered to no less than men and women.

The Jains who deal with the creatures (and with laymen)
wear white, while their more enterprising hermit brothers
are called the *sky-clad* and walk naked. Jains pray
to no deity, kindness being their sole illusion.

Mahavira and those twenty-three other airy creatures
who became saints with him, preached the doctrine of *ahimsa*,
which in our belligerent tongue becomes *non-violence*.
It is not a doctrine congenial to the snarers and poultrymen
who bring to market every day maimed pheasants.
Some of these are bought by their Jain brothers
and brought, to grow back their wing-tips and illusions,
to one of the hospitals maintained for such victims.

When strong and feathered again, the lucky victims
get reborn, on Sunday mornings, to all the world's violence,
set free from the rooftops of these temples of illusion.
It is hard for westerners to speak about men and women
like these, who call the birds of the air their brothers.
We recall the embarrassed fanfare for St. Francis and his
     smalle foules.

We're poor, forked, sky-clad things ourselves
and God knows prey to illuson. *E. g.,* I claim these brothers
and sisters in India, stemming a little violence, among birds.

NOTES ON CONTRIBUTORS

MARGARET CHATTERJEE is Professor of Philosophy, Delhi University, and Vice President of the International Society for Metaphysics. The author of *Our knowledge of Other Selves* (1963), *Philosophical Enquiries* (1968), *The Existentialist Outlook* (1973), and editor of *Contemporary Indian Philosophy* (1974), her latest book *The language of Philosophy*, appeared in 1981. She has published four volumes of poetry and one of short stories, and papers in *Kant-Studien, Philosophy and Phenomenological Research, The Journal of Aesthetics and Art Criticism, Diogenes, Diotima Religious Studies, Religious Traditions* and other journals.

R.W. DESAI, Professor of English at the University of Delhi, obtained the Ph. D. from Northwestern University. The author of *Yeats's Shakespeare* and *Sir John Falstaff, Knight*, he has two recent articles: 'A Phenomenological interpretation of *The White Devil*', in *English Medieval and Renaissance Drama*, ed. Leeds Barroll, and 'An Analysis of Adam's fall in *Paradise Lost*,' to appear in the December 1983 issue of *Milton Quarterlty*.

WILLIAM MULDER is Professor of English at the University of Utah, Salt Lake City. He has a Ph. D. in the History of American Civilization from Harvard. He served for several years as Director of the American Studies Research Centre in Hyderabad. He is the author of *Homeward to Zion*:

The Mormon Migration from Scandinavia and, with A.R. Mortensen, *Among the Mormons: Historic Accounts by Contemporary Observers.* His articles on aspects of American literature and history have appeared in journals and collections including *The Dictionary of American Biography*, *Harvard Theological Review*, *Atlantic Quarterly*, *American Literature*, and *The Western Humanities Review* which he has also edited.

SUKRITA PAUL KUMAR is a Lecturer in English at Zakir Hussain College, Delhi University. She has a Ph. D. in American fiction from Marathawada University and is currently engaged on a comparative study of the modern Indian short story with its English and American counterparts. She has published several poems including a book entitled *Oscillations.*

RUBY CHATTERJI is a Reader in English at Delhi University. She holds M.A. degrees from Calcutta and Leicester Universities and a Ph. D. from the University of Cambridge. She has published important articles on drama in reputed international journals including *Renaissance Drama* (Northwestern University, Illinois), *Studies in English Literature* (Rice University, Texas), *Notes and Queries* (Oxford). She is currently writing a book on Thomas Middleton.

LALITA SUBBU is a Lecturer in English in Hindu College, Delhi University. She has recently received the M. Phil, degree from Delhi University. She is also an accomplished singer of Eastern and Western classical and modern songs and has regular programmes on All India Radio.

MALASHRI LAL is a Lecturer in Jesus and Mary College, Delhi University. She has submitted her thesis on Henry James to the University of Rajasthan for the Ph. D. degree.

J.N. SHARMA is Professor and Head of the Department of English, University of Jodhpur. He obtained his Ph. D. from Indiana. He is the author of *The International Fiction of Henry James* (1979); he has written Introduction and Notes to *The Portrait of a Lady* and co-edited *Contemporary*

American Life (1981).   He has also published essays on Henry James, T.S. Eliot, Lionel Trilling, Hemingway, Saul Bellow in professional journals.

AMRITJIT SINGH is Professor of the Department of English, University of Rajasthan, Jaipur.   He received his Ph. D. from New York University.   Singh is the author of *The Novels of the Harlem Renaissance* (Penn State University Press, 1976) and co-editor of *Afro-American Poetry and Drama, 1760-1975* and *Indian Literature in English, 1827-1979,* published by Gale Research Co. Detroit. Recently Singh has been guest editor of a special number of *New Letters* (Kansas City) on Contemporary Indian writing.

JACOB SLOAN who was formerly an editor of *Span,* USICA, Delhi, has now returned to the U.S.A.   His article on *The Autobiography of Malcolm X* appeared in 1970.   He is the author of a book of poetry, *Generation of Journey,* and has edited several important historical memoirs, notably, Emmanuel Ringleblum's *Notes from the Warsaw Ghetto.*

KUMKUM SANGARI is a Lecturer in Indra Prastha College, Delhi University. She received her Ph. D. from Leeds University working on Scott Fitzgerald and Henry James.

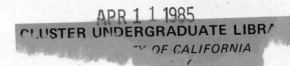